Palgrave Socio-Legal Studies

Series Editor
Dave Cowan, School of Law, University of Bristol, Bristol, UK

Editorial Board
Dame Hazel Genn, University College London, London, UK
Fiona Haines, School of Social & Political Sciences, University of Melbourne, Melbourne, VIC, Australia
Herbert Kritzer, University of Minnesota, Minneapolis, MN, USA
Linda Mulcahy, Centre for Socio-Legal Studies, University of Oxford, Oxford, UK
Rosemary Hunter, Kent Law School, University of Kent, Canterbury, UK
Carl Stychin, Institute of Advanced Legal Studies, University of London, London, UK
Mariana Valverde, Centre for Criminology & Socio-Legal Studies, University of Toronto, Toronto, ON, Canada
Sally Wheeler, College of Law, Australian National University, Canberra, ACT, Australia
Senthorun Raj, Manchester Metropolitan University, Manchester, Lancashire, UK

The Palgrave Socio-Legal Studies series is a developing series of monographs and textbooks featuring cutting edge work which, in the best tradition of socio-legal studies, reach out to a wide international audience.

Amanda Byer

Placing Property

A Legal Geography of Property Rights in Land

Amanda Byer
Sutherland School of Law
University College Dublin
Dublin, Ireland

ISSN 2947-9274 ISSN 2947-9282 (electronic)
Palgrave Socio-Legal Studies
ISBN 978-3-031-31993-8 ISBN 978-3-031-31994-5 (eBook)
https://doi.org/10.1007/978-3-031-31994-5

© The Editor(s) (if applicable) and The Author(s) 2023. This book is an open access publication.

Open Access This book is licensed under the terms of the Creative Commons Attribution 4.0 International License (http://creativecommons.org/licenses/by/4.0/), which permits use, sharing, adaptation, distribution and reproduction in any medium or format, as long as you give appropriate credit to the original author(s) and the source, provide a link to the Creative Commons license and indicate if changes were made.
The images or other third party material in this book are included in the book's Creative Commons license, unless indicated otherwise in a credit line to the material. If material is not included in the book's Creative Commons license and your intended use is not permitted by statutory regulation or exceeds the permitted use, you will need to obtain permission directly from the copyright holder.
The use of general descriptive names, registered names, trademarks, service marks, etc. in this publication does not imply, even in the absence of a specific statement, that such names are exempt from the relevant protective laws and regulations and therefore free for general use.
The publisher, the authors, and the editors are safe to assume that the advice and information in this book are believed to be true and accurate at the date of publication. Neither the publisher nor the authors or the editors give a warranty, expressed or implied, with respect to the material contained herein or for any errors or omissions that may have been made. The publisher remains neutral with regard to jurisdictional claims in published maps and institutional affiliations.

Cover illustration: © Harvey Loake

This Palgrave Macmillan imprint is published by the registered company Springer Nature Switzerland AG
The registered company address is: Gewerbestrasse 11, 6330 Cham, Switzerland

Preface

This book is the result of postdoctoral research undertaken as part of a subproject investigating the origins and development of land as property within the Property [In]Justice project. Property [In]justice (2020–2025) is supported by the European Research Council (ERC) under the European Union's Horizon 2020 research and innovation programme, grant agreement No. 853514. The project investigates the role of international law in creating spatial justice and injustice through its conception of property rights in land. The project expands traditional legal analysis to include interdisciplinary and cross-cultural perspectives and aims to push the boundaries of property and advocate for more place-based understandings of land across international law. The project is led by Professor Amy Strecker, and hosted by the Sutherland School of Law, University College Dublin.

Diverse non-ownership interests in land predate the current institution of private property rights, yet international law, which claims to be universal, appears to give priority to one interpretation of property, derived from the common law. Placing Property takes this premise as its starting point, adopting a legal geographical analysis of property's conceptual foundations in the common law, uniting cultural and environmental critiques of property in law and geography, and considering the effects of property rights on the cultural dimension of land, across a range of communities, Indigenous and non-Indigenous. The law's role in constituting property in detachment from land is an underlying theme, and this work is meant to both ground and bridge property analyses concerned with confronting the transnational effects of property law on land.

My gratitude to the School of Law, University College Dublin, where this research was conducted, and the academic community, including colleagues and staff on campus, for providing such a welcoming environment—during a pandemic no less! I am indebted to Professor Amy Strecker, Principal Investigator of the Property [In]Justice project for her support and encouragement, for believing in this work and her sound advice as to its potential—right on all fronts, Amy! Thank you to the Property [In]justice team—fellow legal geography comrades Sonya Cotton, Sinéad Mercier, and Raphael Ng'etich read and commented on the draft at various stages. Deirdre Norris was invaluable during the publishing process. And a special thank you to Nicole Graham and Kenneth Olwig for reviewing the final draft—'Placing Property' owes much to their pioneering scholarship in the legal and cultural geography fields respectively.

Thanks are due to Palgrave Macmillan/Springer Nature, especially Josephine Taylor, Senior Commissioning Editor, Criminology & Socio-Legal Studies for her positive response to 'Placing Property' and Dave Cowan, Shreenidhi Natarajan and Bhavya Rattan for their assistance during the publishing process. I am also grateful to the anonymous reviewers, whose in-depth comments enabled me to refine aspects of my argument and strengthen the draft, and the Editing Press for providing editorial assistance via a Laura Bassi Junior Academic Scholarship.

Finally, thank you to the European Research Council (ERC), under the EU's Horizon 2020 research and innovation programme, grant agreement no. 853514, whose funding made the publication of this work possible.

Dublin, Ireland
January 2023

Amanda Byer

Acknowledgements

This book has been supported by the European Research Council (ERC) under the European Union's Horizon 2020 research and innovation programme, grant agreement No. 853514. The Property [In]Justice project (2020–2025) is funded by the ERC and investigates the role of international law in creating spatial justice and injustice through its conception of property rights in land. In going beyond traditional legal analysis to include interdisciplinary and cross-cultural perspectives, the project aims to push the boundaries of property and advocate for more place-based understandings of land across international law. The project is led by Professor Amy Strecker, and hosted by the Sutherland School of Law, University College Dublin. The content of this publication does not reflect the official opinion of the European Union. Responsibility for the information and views expressed therein lies entirely with the author.

This project has received funding from the European Research Council (ERC), under the EU's Horizon 2020 research and innovation programme, grant agreement no. 853514

PRAISE FOR *Placing Property*

"This wonderfully readable and timely book takes readers on an intellectually compelling tour of land rights, customs, and practices across an impressive range of landscapes including pre-feudal Scandinavia, pre-Columbian America, the colonisation of the Caribbean and Ireland... Byer powerfully demonstrates the need to embed land laws within their geographical conditions and limits."
—Nicole Graham, Professor and Associate Dean Education, Sydney Law School, The University of Sydney, Australia; author of *Lawscape: Property, Law, Environment* (Routledge, 2011)

"This book uniquely brings together the usually disconnected domains of landscape, law, place, property and justice into a cohesive whole. This will become an invaluable source to readers seeking a comprehensive understanding of the contemporary scholarly questioning that is unsettling the once so seemingly settled absolute right of property."
—Kenneth R. Olwig, Emeritus Professor of Landscape Architecture, Swedish University of Agricultural Science, Alnarp

Contents

1 Introduction: A Legal Geography of Property Rights in Land ... 1
2 Placing Property in the Landscape ... 7
3 Locke and the Homogenisation of the Landscape ... 17
4 Blackstone and the Externalisation of Landscape ... 27
5 Marx and the Dephysicalisation of the Landscape ... 37
6 Extinguishing Landscape, Creating Property: Property and Spatial Injustice ... 53
7 Progressive Property: A Spatially Just Approach to Property? ... 59
8 Conclusion: Property's Placelessness ... 65

Index ... 69

About the Author

Amanda Byer is a postdoctoral researcher in the ERC-funded Property [In]Justice Project based at the Sutherland School of Law, University College Dublin. She holds a Ph.D. in Cultural Heritage Law from Leiden University, the Netherlands, and an LL.M. in Environmental Law from University College London. Amanda's research interests lie at the intersection of landscape, law and spatial justice, engaging aspects of environmental law, cultural heritage law and property law. Her doctoral research (monograph published with Sidestone Press, 2022) involved a legal geographical analysis of heritage, planning and environmental laws in the English-speaking Caribbean (Lesser Antilles) and considered the importance of land's cultural dimension to heritage protection. Previously, Amanda was a postdoctoral fellow at the New York University School of Law, where she explored the role of the Escazú Agreement on Access to Information, Public Participation and Justice in Environmental Matters in Latin America and the Caribbean in building legal institutions for climate resilient development in small island developing states.

CHAPTER 1

Introduction: A Legal Geography of Property Rights in Land

Abstract The opening chapter sets out the aim of the work, which is to examine the common law concept of property in relation to land using a landscape lens. The chapter distinguishes this research from other genealogies of property by emphasising the use of the legal geography methodology to critique property in terms of its relation to space. The chapter summarises the main features of modern land law. The book's structure is outlined, beginning with an exploration of property's roots in landscape, an investigation of the development of the classic hallmarks of property through a legal geographical analysis of classic property theory, a discussion of property's linkages to spatial injustice and a critique of progressive property's potential to challenge the ownership paradigm in property law.

Keywords Common law · Property · Landscape · Legal geography · Spatial justice

Land undergirds human existence, providing the material conditions for sustenance, shelter and quality of life. The human past reveals a variety of practices and strategies for land use, given the diversity and instability of environments over time. It is therefore remarkable that land today is classified according to one main characteristic: ownership. Private property rights insofar as they refer to land are defined by the exclusive ownership of a bundle of rights that can be transferred by title. The legal title holder of such rights can thus exclude any non-member from the use and benefit of the land.[1] In both the common law and civil law systems, ius abutendi grants the owner the right to neglect and abuse property, which conflicts with the sustainable governance of resources[2] and notions of integrating planetary limits in policy-making.[3]

Private property was not the dominant form of land use around the world, or even in England, until about 1800.[4] As Rachael Walsh and Lorna Fox O'Mahony note, the '1925 legislation',[5] a suite of consolidating statutes establishing the 'modern' framework for land ownership in England, eliminated 'the features associated with the aristocratic, status-based land system, in favour of capitalist, contract-based free trade in land…Land was re-configured as a fungible commodity, as readily exchangeable as any other'.[6] In the transition to a market-based concept of property rights, informal and unregistered claims to land were unacknowledged. Today, property in land can be defined as land, or a right to the land, or a social utility, leading Kevin Gray and Susan Gray to conclude that 'few concepts are quite so fragile, so elusive and so often misused as the idea of property'.[7]

It is with these informal understandings of land disregarded by the 1925 legislation and modern land law more generally that this book is occupied, as they are directly linked to the amorphous nature of property, its present-day contradictions and incompatibilities. Current property law texts agree with Gray and Gray, admitting that classic property theory rests on precarious conceptual foundations.[8] Nevertheless, this position has been qualified by Alison Clarke, noting that land law was incrementally developed in England with no seismic changes[9]; no particular interest prevailed once the system was

---

[1] Kevin Gray and Susan Francis Gray, 'The Idea of Property in Land' in Susan Bright and John K Dewar (eds), *Land Law: Themes and Perspectives* (Oxford University Press 1998) 15–51, 20.

[2] Margaret Davies (2020) 'Can Property Be Justified in an Entangled World?' *Globalizations* 17(7): 1104–1117, 1105. https://doi.org/10.1080/14747731.2019.1650696.

[3] Kate Raworth, *Doughnut Economics: Seven Ways to Think Like a 21st Century Economist* (Random House 2017).

[4] Martti Koskenniemi (2017) 'Sovereignty, Property and Empire: Early Modern English Contexts' *Theoretical Inquiries in Law* 18: 355–389, 355.

[5] Law of Property Act 1925, Land Charges Act 1925, Land Registration Act 1925, Settled Land Act 1925, Administration of Estates Act 1925.

[6] Rachael Walsh and Lorna Fox O'Mahony, 'Land Law, Property Ideologies and the British-Irish Relationship' (2018) *Common Law World Review* 47(1): 1–25, 12. See also Martin Dixon, *Modern Land Law* (Taylor and Francis 2018).

[7] Gray and Gray 15.

[8] Alison Clarke, *Principles of Property Law* (Cambridge University Press 2020) 5, 12, 17 and at 176, noting that property as private ownership is too narrow and outmoded a category for the range of interests in land, propertisation is not required for full use and control, and though land is a universal resource, it is subject to different cultures living in different environments.

[9] Clarke, *Principles of Property Law* 178.

rationalised[10]; and former colonies adapted the common law to local conditions.[11] This restates the common law stance in modern terms. What Gray and Gray, Clarke, and other property lawyers and scholars have all acknowledged is that property has diverged from land in a complex historical process. Yet, despite legal innovations to promote sustainable land use today, modern legal conceptions of property have proven unable to address the realities of land-driven crises such as pollution, climate change and the pressures of globalisation, and in many cases, enables them.

What was erased by the 1925 Act was not just an antiquated system of tenures, to be replaced by a modern land registration system, but ways of seeing and understanding land defined by features and processes, rather than boundaries; specifically, the relationships communities developed in interaction with their environs, and the customs generated to maintain those relationships and a way of life. Known as landscape, this cultural geographical descriptor of place implied a distinct locality that connected community, land and law for centuries and functioned as a rubric for diverse non-proprietary interests in land.[12]

This book uses the landscape lens to trace the emergence of property in English land law and the common law system, as it diverged from a cluster of place-derived interests to assume its current placeless iteration. 'Placing' property is twofold in meaning: contextualising property as the concept evolved in the development of real property law; and describing location-based understandings of land, in which complementary and competing spatial definitions of land represented viable non-ownership interests shaped by their material conditions—the landscapes of Great Britain, Ireland, the Americas and the Caribbean in particular. The book is therefore both a genealogy and legal geography of property, expanding previous property scholarship that charted the historical development of the term as it emerged from court records, or considered the concept indirectly in relation to the development of the common law.[13]

---

[10] Ibid 180.

[11] Ibid 184.

[12] Amy Strecker, *Landscape Protection in International Law* (Oxford University Press 2017) 185.

[13] David Seipp, 'The Concept of Property in the Early Common Law' (1994) *Law and History Review* 12(1): 29–91; Robert C. Ellickson, 'Property in Land' (1993) *The Yale Law Journal* 102(6): 1315–1400; Kenneth J. Vandevelde, 'The New Property of the Nineteenth Century: The Development of the Modern Concept of Property' (1980) *Buffalo Law Review* 29: 325–368; Robert C Palmer 'The Origins of Property in England' (1985) *Law and History Review* 3(1): 1–50; David A. Thomas, 'Origins of the Common Law (A Three-Part Series) Part I: The Disappearance of Roman Law from Dark Age Britain' (1984) *Buffalo Law Review* 563–599; 'Origins of the Common Law (A Three Part Series)—Part II: Anglo-Saxon Antecedents of the Common Law' (1985) *Buffalo Law Review* 453–504; 'Origins of the Common Law (A Three-Part Series) Part III: Common Law Under the Early Normans' (1986) *Buffalo Law Review* 109–127; George Burton Adams, 'The Origin of the Common Law' (1924) *The Yale Law Journal* 34(2): 115–128.

This spatial reading of property examines the geographical origins of the legal concept and its impact on specific places. Legal geography conceives of a broader understanding of the law beyond its doctrinal foundations, to uncover spatial assumptions and biases that are accepted or ignored.[14] Formal law may derive much of its (often silent) ideology and values from pre-existing systems of lore and norms that are spatially located, influencing its development and implementation.[15] Specifically, legal geography engages law's presumed neutrality in the context of 'spatial blindness',[16] and asks how established legal categories such as property can be reconciled with the reality of geography.[17] This requires integrating the material conditions of specific places into the law. As Robyn Bartel et al. have noted, ignoring geography has political consequences; if we do not ask questions about the location of law's impact, and therefore who it impacts, then its effects, such as environmental destruction or the dispossession and genocide of Indigenous peoples, may be dismissed.[18] Geographically sensitive rules thus make the law relevant and capable of delivering spatial justice. Legal geography is also cognisant of the historical context, examining material conditions, limits and connections over time.[19]

In the first chapter, property's origins are explicated, followed by a discussion of the key developments in the conceptualisation of land as property, as the common law system gradually retreated from grounded perspectives on land in favour of abstract rights that are individual, exclusive and alienable—the so-called classic indicia or hallmarks of property. The contributions of Locke, Blackstone and Marx are each analysed in relation to the classic hallmark of property with which they correspond. The implications of private property as the outcome of the legal extinguishment of the landscape are then discussed in the context of spatial injustice. I address briefly the potential of the progressive property school to contribute to a more spatially just concept of property before concluding with some final thoughts.

---

[14] Antonia Layard 'Reading Law Spatially' in Naomi Creutzfeldt, Marc Mason and Kirsten McConnachie (eds), *Routledge Handbook of Socio-Legal Theory and Methods* (Routledge 2019) 233.

[15] Robyn Bartel, Nicole Graham, Sue Jackson, Jason Hugh Prior, Daniel Francis Robinson, Meg Sherval and Stewart Williams, 'Legal Geography: An Australian Perspective' (November 2013) *Geographical Research* 51(4): 339–353, 346.

[16] Antonia Layard, 'What Is Legal Geography?' (*University of Bristol Law School Blog*, 11 April 2016), http://legalresearch.blogs.bris.ac.uk/2016/04/what-is-legal-geography/, accessed 11 May 2021.

[17] Layard 'Reading Law Spatially' 237.

[18] Bartel et al., 341.

[19] Ibid 349.

References

GB Adams, 'The Origin of the Common Law' (1924) *The Yale Law Journal* 34(2): 115–128.

R Bartel, N Graham, S Jackson, JH Prior, DF Robinson, M Sherval and S Williams, 'Legal Geography: An Australian Perspective' (November 2013) *Geographical Research* 51(4): 339–353.

S Bright and JK Dewar (eds), *Land Law: Themes and Perspectives* (Oxford University Press 1998).

A Clarke, *Principles of Property Law* (Cambridge University Press 2020).

N Creutzfeldt, M Mason and K McConnachie (eds), *Routledge Handbook of Socio-Legal Theory and Methods* (Routledge 2019).

M Davies 'Can Property Be Justified in an Entangled World?' (2020) *Globalizations* 17(7): 1104–1117.

M Dixon, *Modern Land Law* (Taylor and Francis 2018).

RC Ellickson, 'Property in Land' (1993) *The Yale Law Journal* 102(6): 1315–1400.

M Koskenniemi (2017) 'Sovereignty, Property and Empire: Early Modern English Contexts' *Theoretical Inquiries in Law* 18: 355–389.

A Layard, 'What Is Legal Geography?' (*University of Bristol Law School Blog* 11 April 2016), accessed 11 May 2021, http://legalresearch.blogs.bris.ac.uk/2016/04/what-is-legal-geography/.

RC Palmer 'The Origins of Property in England' (1985) *Law and History Review* 3(1): 1–50.

K Raworth, *Doughnut Economics: Seven Ways to Think Like a 21st Century Economist* (Random House 2017).

D Seipp, 'The Concept of Property in the Early Common Law' (1994) *Law and History Review* 12(1): 29–91.

A Strecker, *Landscape Protection in International Law* (Oxford University Press 2017).

DA Thomas, 'Origins of the Common Law (A Three-Part Series) Part I: The Disappearance of Roman Law from Dark Age Britain' (1984) *Brigham Young University Law Review* 4: 563–599.

———, 'Origins of the Common Law (A Three-Part Series) Part II: Anglo-Saxon Antecedents of the Common Law' (1985) *Brigham Young University Law Review* 3: 453–504.

———, 'Origins of the Common Law (A Three-Part Series) Part III: Common Law Under the Early Normans' (1986) *Brigham Young University Law Review* 1: 109–127.

KJ Vandevelde, 'The New Property of the Nineteenth Century: The Development of the Modern Concept of Property' (1980) *Buffalo Law Review* 29: 325–368.

R Walsh and L Fox O'Mahony, 'Land Law, Property Ideologies and the British-Irish Relationship' (2018) *Common Law World Review* 47(1): 1–25.

Open Access This chapter is licensed under the terms of the Creative Commons Attribution 4.0 International License (http://creativecommons.org/licenses/by/4.0/), which permits use, sharing, adaptation, distribution and reproduction in any medium or format, as long as you give appropriate credit to the original author(s) and the source, provide a link to the Creative Commons license and indicate if changes were made.

The images or other third party material in this chapter are included in the chapter's Creative Commons license, unless indicated otherwise in a credit line to the material. If material is not included in the chapter's Creative Commons license and your intended use is not permitted by statutory regulation or exceeds the permitted use, you will need to obtain permission directly from the copyright holder.

CHAPTER 2

Placing Property in the Landscape

Abstract To explain property's origins in place or landscape, this chapter draws on legal, historical, geographical, etymological and archaeological research to reconstruct how people understood land before property. The chapter relies on two main sources: Kenneth Olwig's cultural geographical research on early landscapes in pre-feudal Scandinavia and Sub-Roman/pre-enclosure Britain illustrates the relationship between land, law and people; and Nicole Graham's etymological analysis linking property not to ownership but to proximity affirms that a specific location to which someone belonged generated relations relevant to identity, community and a sustainable way of life. Land was communal, dynamic and characterised by attachment, the polar opposite of property's defining characteristics today (individual, exclusive and alienable).

Keywords Landscape · Place · Propriety · Custom · Identity · Graham · Olwig

Legal historians have noted that traditional analyses of property rights tend to begin with the English Whig philosopher John Locke, rarely focusing on the meaning, scope or importance of property in the centuries of common law development predating Locke, and this is significant because the modern lawyer's concept of property would have been unrecognisable to those early practitioners.[1] We, therefore, begin before property, focusing primarily on

---

[1] Seipp 30.

Kenneth Olwig's work on landscapes,[2] Nicole Graham's research on property, environment and law,[3] as well as archaeological and etymological scholarship, to paint a picture of land in the centuries preceding the Norman conquest of England.

As discussed earlier, private property is of recent construction. Archaeological evidence has indicated that open field systems were in use in Britain for hundreds of years before the Anglo-Saxons arrived in the fifth century.[4] Land managed in common afforded communities the opportunity to work together to protect resources and sustain their families. The particular character of cattle grazing and crop planting generated cooperative practices, which later formed the basis of customary law. Institutions were created to embed, defend and amend this locally acquired knowledge for future generations. This system was overlaid and adapted by successive communities throughout the island's history,[5] and hybrid communities may have arisen, based on archaeological and place-name evidence in the fenlands for example.[6]

The words 'land', 'landscipe' and 'landsceap' enter early English through the Anglo-Saxon language.[7] The link between ideas of customary law, institutions embodying that law, and the people enfranchised to participate in the making and administration of law was fundamental to the root 'land', which was not dissimilar to our word country, with its own legal system and representative council.[8] The primary meaning of land attached to a farm

[2] Kenneth Olwig, *Landscape, Nature and the Body Politic: From Britain's Renaissance to America's New World* (University of Wisconsin Press 2002).

[3] Nicole Graham, *Lawscape: Property, Environment, Law* (Routledge-Cavendish 2010).

[4] Susan Oosthuizen, 'Recognizing and Moving on from a Failed Paradigm: The Case of Agricultural Landscapes in Anglo-Saxon England c. AD 400–800' (June 2016) *Journal of Archaeological Research* 24(2): 179–227, 214. Oosthuizen states that the archaeological record calls into question the accepted premise that common property rights were an Anglo-Saxon innovation; it is possible that they were a traditional form of governance in early medieval England, inherited from a prehistoric and Romano-British past.

[5] Oosthuizen 216. The boundaries of prehistoric and Roman pastures are often marked by definitive earthworks that were used during the Anglo-Saxon period. The areas within them, apparently grazed (since there is no evidence of arable cultivation), were not subdivided into smaller units as might be expected for individual households, suggesting that flocks and herds were collectively managed. This implies that graziers needed to collectively manage the outer boundaries of the pasture, govern rights of access, regulate seasonal access to ensure equitable exploitation, manage disputes and so on. Substantial prehistoric gatherings are well evidenced archaeologically, timed to coincide with the arrival and/or departure of the animals when disputes about rights to grazing and ownership of stock were most likely to occur.

[6] Susan Oosthuizen, 'Culture and Identity in the Early Medieval Fenland Landscape' (2016) *Landscape History* 37(1): 5–24, 5. https://doi.org/10.1080/01433768.2016.1176433.

[7] Joseph Bosworth, 'Land-Scipe'; 'Land-Sceap'. In An Anglo-Saxon Dictionary Online, edited by Thomas Northcote Toller, Christ Sean, and Ondřej Tichy. Prague: Faculty of Arts, Charles University, 2014, https://bosworthtoller.com/21128; https://bosworthtoller.com/21126 accessed 5 December 2020.

[8] Olwig, *Landscape, Nature and the Body Politic* 17.

or manor or cultivated land such as a common or meadow, and in feudal Europe, these lands were not separate properties owned by individuals, but complexes of use rights that were determined by custom and personal feudal obligations. These lands, taken together, could constitute larger lands under a given body of law with ancient origins predating feudalism.[9] Where lands were more challenging to inhabit, and required specialised knowledge and complex systems of organisation, there were less likely to be manors and so, they evolved to be more autonomous in character—peasant republics and flexible alternatives to centralised states.[10] This distinguished a landscape from an administrative unit, as there was more independent internal development, and this gave the landscape's inhabitants a greater right to self-determination and participation.[11]

'Land' was therefore a system of nested obligations, use rights and institutions representing a people and its relationship with the material environs. Its cognates 'landscipe' and 'landsceap' illuminate this relationship, as they refer to ship or shape. They denote both the role of the people in shaping the land, giving it its unique physical or cultural character, the character of the land itself in influencing the practices and livelihoods of those people in a dynamic mutually constitutive process and the shape or form the abstract quality of this relationship assumed. Ship, as in fellowship, signified the abstract qualities generated by the people working the land together, informing the values and beliefs that bound them together, and provided the moral content for the representation inhabitants of the land received for working the land together. This representation was embodied in the institutions developed to protect these customary rules and rights, in open-air assemblies or things, and the rules and practices they developed, informed by the land and generated by their association with each other, became their locally derived laws.[12]

Law is thus an inherent element of the landscape. As Olwig writes, the ancient Germanic name for the representative legal and political body of a land was the thing or moot—the root of the modern words 'thing' and 'meeting'.[13] It is the deliberation of the thing that builds the land as a polity or res publica (transliterated 'public thing'), or landscape. This interplay between

---

[9] Ibid.

[10] Ibid 15.

[11] Ibid 11.

[12] Kenneth Olwig, 'Representation and Alienation in the Political Landscape' (2005) *Cultural Geographies* 12(1): 19–40, 20: 'Landscape' is distinguished from land by the suffix -scape, which is equivalent in function to the more common English suffix -ship, and this suffix generates an abstraction. Thus, as Olwig explains, there might be two friends, comrades or fellows in a room, both concrete beings, but between them they share something abstract and difficult to define: friendship, comradeship or fellowship; it is the suffix -ship which designates this abstract quality, the nature, state or constitution of being a friend, and these qualities in turn are linked together by Olwig to draw attention to their concretised and institutionalised counterparts (nature, the state and a constitution).

[13] Olwig, 'Representation and Alienation' 22.

land, community practice and its institutionalised relationship thus renders the landscape a political one, and situates the power of the representative body in custom.[14]

Landscipe in the Old English spelling[15] is derived from the Germanic family of languages: Dutch landschap, Danish landskab, Swedish landskap and German landschaft.[16] It refers to the land, its character, traditions or customs.[17] The landschaften of Angeln and Frisia from Germany and Denmark produced the settlers who pushed the Britons north and gave England its Anglo-Saxon identity.[18] As noted earlier, archaeological evidence indicates that they could very well have adopted British land practices, for communal land use was already extant in the Celtic world.[19]

This is the context in which land use and ownership arose in England. The landschaft was a community of law,[20] with its own representative council or ting, as in Jutland in Denmark. The institution of the ting was also found in England where it was known as the moot. The Danish land was divided into herreder, each with its own ting, much as the English shire or county (such as Northumberland) was divided into hundreds. Other historic shires and areas with the suffix -land or -folk (Cumberland, Westmoreland, Suffolk, Norfolk) provide evidence of once-autonomous areas in England.[21] All important decisions binding the community were made at this assembly, also functioning as a court, and as a mechanism communicating between local communities and central authorities.[22] Custom and culture, therefore, defined the land as a social entity that found physical expression in the area under its law.[23]

The common law thus originated in local custom. At the beginning of the 1100 s, the English legal system was pluralistic, fragmented and decentralised.

---

[14] Ibid.
[15] Olwig, 'Representation and Alienation' 22.
[16] Olwig, *Landscape, Nature and the Body Politic* 232.
[17] Ibid 18.
[18] Olwig 10–11.
[19] The rundale communal land system potentially predates the Norman Conquest and the centralised system of land tenure that would be imposed on Irish society. As a distinct pattern of land use that had existed for at least 200 years prior to the Famine, it is associated with the development of Celtic Ireland. Rúndale is a term derived from two Gaelic words: 'roinn', which refers to a sharing or division of something, and 'dail' which usually refers to a meeting or assembly. A rúndale was a meeting where members of a peasant community or clachan met to distribute and redistribute land. Clachan land was known as rundale, and this communal ownership of land, and distribution of social product was based on shared lineage and lineage mode of production. See Dean M. Braa, 'The Great Potato Famine and the Transformation of Irish Peasant Society' (1997) *Science & Society* 61(2): 193–215, 200–201.
[20] Olwig, *Landscape Nature and Body Politic* 20.
[21] Ibid 49.
[22] Ibid 17.
[23] Ibid.

Jurisdiction was largely based on medieval political units—the shire, hundred or borough. From the tenth century onwards, each of these jurisdictions had been nominally under the supervisory control of the King.[24] Until the eighteenth century, jurisdiction was predominantly organised by subject-matter or personal status: ecclesiastical courts determined matters relating to church law, manorial courts applied the body of customary law known as manorial law to matters concerning village life and forestry courts oversaw the body of law known as the law of the forest.[25]

Land use in Anglo-Saxon England was thus far more diverse and flexible and modes of succession demonstrate this.[26] Bookland (bocland) and folkland (folcland), were used to describe all land in Anglo-Saxon England, but the words themselves are rare in Anglo-Saxon documents.[27] Bookland is believed to refer to land granted by royal boc, or charter, while folkland addressed everything else, including inherited land and common land. Another category, family land, has been suggested.[28] Early laws indicate that these categories were fluid, and relied on the public assemblies or courts to modify succession arrangements and mediate disputes. The regular meetings of the shire and hundred would have provided the ideal forum for these declarations.[29] Such land use systems were therefore not primitive or idyllic in character. They were flexible, in order to accommodate the layered and socially complex structures of their communities, where common property rights coexisted with, complemented, qualified and enhanced existing or nascent 'vertical' hierarchies of all kinds, whether social, religious, political or economic.[30]

These landscapes could adapt and reinvent themselves, even in challenging environments such as the fenlands, where bylaws were preserved in oral traditions of custom and practice to ensure equitable distribution of shared

---

[24] Shaunnagh Dorsett 'Since Time Immemorial: A Story of Common Law Jurisdiction, Native Title and the Case of Tanistry' (2002) *Melbourne University Law Review* 26: 32–59, 36.

[25] Dorsett at 34 and 36.

[26] Julie Mumby, 'The Descent of Family Land in Later Anglo-Saxon England' (2011) *Historical Research* 84(225): 399–415.

[27] According to Julie Mumby, folkland appears only twice: (1) The will of Ealdorman Alfred (871 X 899) (P. H. Sawyer, Anglo-Saxon Charters: an Annotated List and Bibliography (1968) available online at http://www.esawyer.org.uk/ accessed 19 October 2020; (2) 'The wife's lament', l. 47 (A Guide to Old English, ed. B Mitchell and FC Robinson [7th edn., Oxford 2007] 276–279). For all 47 occurrences of bookland, see University of Toronto, Dictionary of Old English Web Corpus, http://www.doe.utoronto.ca/index.html accessed 19 October 2020. 'Folkland' and 'bookland' only appear three times in the same document—see Mumby 399, and Paul Vinogradoff, 'Folkland' (1893) *The English Historical Review* 8(29): 1–17, 1.

[28] Mumby 399.

[29] Ibid 404 and at 414.

[30] Susan Oosthuizen, 'Beyond Hierarchy: Archaeology, Common Rights and Social Identity' (2016) *World Archaeology* 48(3): 381–394, 385.

resources.[31] This did not preclude interaction with hierarchical structures, and certainly, the arrival of the Normans marked the beginning of the feudal period in England and changes to procedures in land use. As Shaunnagh Dorsett notes, the law was very much in flux at this time, flanked by alternative, and eventually, competing jurisdictions. The pre-Norman divisions of shire, hundred or borough survived the Norman Conquest and continued to function. Each had separate courts, but commonly overlapping jurisdictions.[32]

Nevertheless, control over land did not signify ownership in the modern sense. Feudal lords did not possess land as property, as was the case under the Roman law of possessio. Feudal ties to the land were developed through interpersonal relations of fealty, whereas the customary law, which guaranteed access to the commons, was the expression of particular local and national communities.[33] The lord's seigneurial rights were therefore not absolute, and merely one of an array of interests that were place-determined.[34] As David Seipp writes, land was different: 'land meant an army could be raised; it sustained overlapping claims and casual and regular uses, and was therefore treated differently in the courts, unlike property claims in goods and animals'.[35]

We can see how property and landscape intersect when the etymology of property is examined. Graham writes that property originally invoked an integrated relationship between people and place,[36] a relationship that mirrored the connection between people, land and the law in the landscape. This was derived from the Old French 'proprete' from the Latin proprietas meaning, proper to, one's own or special character.[37] The French word 'propre' means clean or suitable in the sense of 'close' or 'near' or 'in place', and the Old French and Latin meanings derived from the Greek 'idiotes', meaning a distinctive or distinguishable quality, the peculiar nature or specific character, and it was the means by which ownership could be claimed—the proximity of the thing to the person was considered sufficiently close so as to be associated

---

[31] Oosthuizen, 'Beyond Hierarchy' 385.
[32] Dorsett 36.
[33] Olwig, *Landscape, Nature and the Body Politic* 53.
[34] Ibid 123.
[35] Seipp 86–87.
[36] Graham 24.
[37] Chambers Dictionary online, https://chambers.co.uk/search/?query=property&title=21st accessed 5 December 2020. Graham 24–27: property originally linked people and place. What was proper to a person were the physical qualities so closely associated with that person that he could be identified with them. Today, the secondary meaning is significant only in the scientific world, e.g. what are the properties of hydrogen. The primary meaning pertains to abstract relations between people, rather than with or over physical things. Today, the dominant feature of property is alienability not identity, inverting the original meaning.

with that person.[38] Real property signified a human relationship with the physical features of the landscape that overrode lesser forms of property (in goods or animals). Real property could not be explicated without this identifying set of geophysical and cultural relations.[39]

Gray and Gray call this a sense of propriety, 'rightness', meaning that property does not derive from any sense of entitlement (enforceable exclusory title).[40] Property linked to identity, because to say something is 'my own' signifies that it forms part of who they are. Because land was an important part of identity in medieval England and the early common law, the location of land was relevant in any dispute, rather than abstract legal categories.[41] Nevertheless it is the secondary meaning of property that prevails today, meaning an interest in having a thing, rather than the attribute or characteristic of a person or thing.[42]

This inversion of property's meaning, from mutual identification to alienability, from attachment to detachment, reflects what Graham describes as the transformation in the way modern Anglo-European relationships between people and place have changed over time.[43] Property is defined not by identification or association with a place, but its alienation from it. This connotes a shift from a mutually defining relationship of ownership and identity to a unilateral relationship of ownership and alienability.[44] Today, property is viewed as abstract entitlements exchanged between persons that are alienable from, rather than proper to a person, no longer attached to or even integrated with the identity of an individual or community.[45] Landscape's demotion is evident by the word's re-entry in the English language in the sixteenth century, associated with landscape painting and gardening, viewing the land from the individual perspective at a distance, based on cartographical and surveying techniques and representation through visual rather than political means.[46]

Land and place had become synonymous with property—by the seventeenth century, the term itself denoted both property and knowing one's

---

[38] Graham 26.

[39] Ibid 25.

[40] Gray and Gray 15: The term 'property' is simply an abbreviated reference to a quantum of socially permissible power exercised in respect of a socially valued resource. Used in this way, the word 'property' reflects its semantically correct root by identifying the condition of a particular resource as being 'proper' to a particular person. In this deeper sense... the language of 'property' may have more in common with 'propriety' than with entitlement; and the notion of a 'property' right may ultimately have more to do with perceptions of 'rightness' than with any understanding of enforceable exclusory title.

[41] Seipp 46, 49 and Graham 26.

[42] Graham 26.

[43] Ibid 25.

[44] Ibid 26.

[45] Ibid 27.

[46] Olwig, 'Representation and Alienation' 23.

place.[47] The historical concept of landscape in the primary substantive sense of place and polity, referring to lands 'scaped' or shaped according to customary law as adjudicated by representative legal assemblies especially influenced English common law.[48] In such a polity, common customary law is primarily enforced through moral pressure and community control (the word 'moral' deriving from the Latin word for mores or customs), so that a customary prescriptive use-right that is neglected or abused automatically extinguishes any moral right to it, and will be lost; this principle ensured the functioning of a working community, and prevented the erosion of a shared-resource system by reinforcing rights held in common for the public good.[49] Sustainability in resource management, representation and social justice thus characterised the working landscape.[50] However, the common law eventually consolidated custom, and in so doing, dismissed locally specific practices that enabled those landscapes to function.

What archaeological, etymological, historical and geographic research indicate is that there were many ways of seeing, defining and regulating land, even as Norman governance concentrated control hierarchically, away from local communities. Nevertheless, the focus on an administrative rather than a legal system meant that customary practices persisted until consolidated in the common law of the realm.[51] This was problematic, as alternative systems of law were replaced.[52] In addition, custom codified in the law neutralised the flexibility inherent in communal land management,[53] which had implications

---

[47] Olwig, *Landscape Nature and Body Politic* 123.

[48] Olwig, 'Virtual Enclosure, Ecosystem Services, Landscape's Character and the 'Rewilding' of the Commons: the 'Lake District' Case' (2016) *Landscape Research* 41(2): 253–264, 256. Representatives of shire courts later formed the basis for the House of Commons.

[49] Ibid.

[50] Olwig, see Susan Oosthuizen, 'Culture and Identity in the Early Medieval Fenland Landscape' (2016) *Landscape History* 37(1): 5–24. https://doi.org/10.1080/01433768.2016.1176433.

[51] William Deller addresses the importance of memory to the medieval mind, noting that oral recollection in court testimony continued to be held in high regard after 1300, with the introduction of written records, and traditional aspects of land use continued to regulate land nearly a century later. See Deller, 'The Transfer of Land in Medieval England from 1246 to 1430: The Language of Acquisition' (2020) *Continuity and Change* 35: 139–162, 143, 157.

[52] English common law would displace the ancient Irish law, Brehon law, in the seventeenth century. A central factor in the conflict was ownership of land and two cases on customary modes of succession, the Case of Tanistry (1608) Day 28; 80 ER 516 and the Case of Gavelkind, 'The Resolution of the Judges, Touching the Irish Custom of Gavelkind' (1608) Dav 49; 80 ER 535; Davies translation, effectively ended the influence of Brehon law. See JCW Wylie, *Wylie on Irish Land Law* (6th edn., Bloomsbury 2020) and Dorsett, 'Since Time Immemorial: A Story of Common Law Jurisdiction, Native Title and the Case of Tanistry' at n 24.

[53] Deller 156. Literacy, documentation and the law permeated the market, supplementing if not supplanting older, communal mentalities like giving and receiving homage,

for community relations and livelihoods and by extension the working landscape.⁵⁴ Many localised jurisdictions or specialist bodies of law, such as lex forestae or the law of the fens, slowly disappeared under the pressure of societal change, leaving behind only those elements that had been accommodated within the framework of the common law. Thus, while lex forestae receded, part of manorial tenure survived, enforced by the common law as the custom of copyhold.⁵⁵

The complexities that surrounded land ensured that inheritance was challenging and land use was often contested, but this was a result of land's responsivity to natural resources in ways that were locally delineated, but never private, exclusive or defined by its alienability. Landscape, therefore, contextualised the meaning or property, since the concept (and the concomitant right) would be rendered meaningless without these place-based connections. Propertising the landscape in the modern sense of the word displaced all other (non-proprietary) interests, as evinced by the crystallisation of the property concept in political economy and the law. This shift from a spatial logic inherent in the landscape to the abstract logic of property would be refined and illustrated in the theories of Locke, Blackstone and Marx.

REFERENCES

DM Braa, 'The Great Potato Famine and the Transformation of Irish Peasant Society' (1997) *Science & Society* 61(2): 193–215.

S Bright and JK Dewar (eds), *Land Law: Themes and Perspectives* (Oxford University Press 1998).

W Deller, 'The Transfer of Land in Medieval England from 1246 to 1430: The Language of Acquisition' (2020) *Continuity and Change* 35: 139–162.

S Dorsett 'Since Time Immemorial: A Story of Common Law Jurisdiction, Native Title and the Case of Tanistry' (2002) *Melbourne University Law Review* 26: 32–59.

N Graham, *Lawscape: Property, Environment, Law* (Routledge-Cavendish 2010).

B Mitchell and FC Robinson (eds), *A Guide to Old English* (7th edn., Oxford 2007).

J Mumby, 'The Descent of Family Land in Later Anglo-Saxon England' (2011) *Historical Research* 84(225): 399–415.

K Olwig, *Landscape, Nature and the Body Politic: From Britain's Renaissance to America's New World* (University of Wisconsin Press 2002).

———, 'Representation and Alienation in the Political Landscape' (2005) *Cultural Geographies* 12(1): 19–40.

---

oral pledges and the witness of the community. Where traditional language like 'enfeoffment' continued to be used the emphasis was on the letter recording the transaction not the face-to-face ceremonial nature of the transfer itself. Possession was foregrounded not deference. While inheritance continued as the bedrock of land acquisition, the legal right of ownership became a key feature of the record rather than unproblematic descent.

⁵⁴ Olwig, *Landscape Nature and the Body Politic* 60.

⁵⁵ Dorsett 41. See also David Tabachnick, 'Two Models of Ownership: How Commons Has Co-Existed with Private Property' (2016) *American Journal of Economics and Sociology* 75(2): 488–563, 493.

———, 'Virtual Enclosure, Ecosystem Services, Landscape's Character and the 'Rewilding' of the Commons: the 'Lake District' Case' (2016) *Landscape Research* 41(2): 253–264.
S Oosthuizen, 'Recognizing and Moving on from a Failed Paradigm: The Case of Agricultural Landscapes in Anglo-Saxon England c. AD 400–800' (June 2016) *Journal of Archaeological Research* 24(2): 179–227.
———, 'Culture and Identity in the Early Medieval Fenland Landscape' (2016) *Landscape History* 37(1): 5–24.
———, 'Beyond Hierarchy: Archaeology, Common Rights and Social Identity' (2016) *World Archaeology* 48(3): 381–394.
D Seipp, 'The Concept of Property in the Early Common Law' (1994) *Law and History Review* 12(1): 29–91.
D Tabachnick, 'Two Models of Ownership: How Commons Has Co-Existed with Private Property' (2016) *American Journal of Economics and Sociology* 75(2): 488–563.
P Vinogradoff, 'Folkland' (1893) *The English Historical Review* 8(29): 1–17.
JCW Wylie, *Wylie on Irish Land Law* (6th edn., Bloomsbury 2020).

Open Access This chapter is licensed under the terms of the Creative Commons Attribution 4.0 International License (http://creativecommons.org/licenses/by/4.0/), which permits use, sharing, adaptation, distribution and reproduction in any medium or format, as long as you give appropriate credit to the original author(s) and the source, provide a link to the Creative Commons license and indicate if changes were made.

The images or other third party material in this chapter are included in the chapter's Creative Commons license, unless indicated otherwise in a credit line to the material. If material is not included in the chapter's Creative Commons license and your intended use is not permitted by statutory regulation or exceeds the permitted use, you will need to obtain permission directly from the copyright holder.

CHAPTER 3

Locke and the Homogenisation of the Landscape

Abstract This chapter examines John Locke's contributions to the property discourse in the context of the first hallmark of property, individuality. A legal geographical analysis of his *Two Treatises* is employed to show how Locke's focus on the individual and the labour theory of value required a reductionist understanding of the commons and communal land use. Locke's influences from improvement philosophy and his role in the colonial administration of North America are also discussed in relation to his understanding of land. The chapter addresses the consequences of perceiving locally developed concepts of common land as empty space or wasteland. Property's association with individual liberty in Anglo-American law is reinterpreted in light of its reliance on and extraction from complex Indigenous landscapes.

Keywords Locke · Two Treatises · Labour theory of value · Commons · Waste · Native Americans · Indigenous landscapes

John Locke's explanation and justification for the acquisition of property is foundational to the common law's treatment of land, but what is absent is a consideration of landscape, particularly Native American landscapes, in the development of that theory. Locke took as his starting point the concept of self-ownership: we have a property in our own person that belongs to no one and no one has right to it.[1] It follows therefore that the labour of our body and the work of our hands are properly ours. Property is created by both

[1] John Locke, *Two Treatises of Government* hereafter *TT* (first published 1689, Hackett Publishing Company 2016) Book II 134: 'every man has a property in his person: this nobody has any right to but himself. The labour of his body, and the work of his hands, we may say is properly his'.

withdrawing land from the commons and adding our labour.[2] The second part of Locke's theory is what Jeremy Waldron calls the labour theory of value—a person adds value to nature.[3] Without labour, land and other natural resources have no value.[4] These two elements of Locke's theory make it clear that land is undistinguished, malleable nature lacking other distinct values (cultural, social and ecological). For Locke, all land is homogenous nature until man creates property by labour, thereby adding value. In making this assumption, Locke 'devalued actual labour of commoners by asserting common property was the same as uncultivated waste'.[5]

The Lockean notion of acquiring private property therefore relied on a concept of nature that was passive and uniform, yet capable of transformation.[6] He states:

> God gave the world to men in common; but since he gave it them for their benefit, and the greatest conveniences of life they were capable to draw from it, it cannot be supposed he meant it should always remain common and uncultivated. He gave it to the use of the industrious and rational, (and labor was to be his title to it) not to the fancy or covetousness of the quarrelsome and contentious.[7]

Locke was not unfamiliar with the many uses to which land had been put in England. In his Two Treatises, he acknowledged the commons but promoted a more individualistic conception of the right to appropriate, linked to an individual's 'self-mastery'—ownership over body and one's actions.[8] This is because, when Locke published his Two Treatises at the end of the seventeenth century, the medieval concept of property associated with status and local custom was subsiding, giving way to ideas about contract and capital[9] and as a result, significant enclosure of land had already begun in order to maximise land's potential, or 'improve' it.[10] The purpose was to stimulate

---

[2] Locke, *TT* Book II 135: Earth is common to all mankind, but man's labour is his own. Whatsoever, then he removes out of the state that nature has provided, and left it in, he has mixed his labor with, and joined to it something that is his own, and thereby makes it his property.
See also Clarke, *Principles of Property Law* 44.

[3] Jeremy Waldron, *The Right to Private Property* (Clarendon Press 1988) 191–194.

[4] Clarke, *Principles of Property Law* 45.

[5] Graham, 86.

[6] Ibid.

[7] Locke, *TT* Book II, 137–138.

[8] Anne C. Dowling, 'Un-Locke-ing a Just Right Environmental Regime: Overcoming the Three Bears of International Environmentalism—Sovereignty, Locke, and Compensation' (2002) *William & Mary Environmental Law and Policy Review* 26: 891–960, 918 on Locke's awareness of nuisance and community-oriented rights.

[9] Graham 48.

[10] Ibid 70.

agrarian development, and so land use and ownership were married, reducing the diversity of interests that once characterised the working landscape in the name of expediency. The primary relationship between people and place was now created through agrarian labour, as opposed to the labour of commoners who engaged in open field practices pre-enclosure.[11] Locke therefore regarded enclosure practices as essential to the implementation of improvement theory and applied this thinking to the appropriation of common property and exclusion of communal rights in England and the Americas.[12]

Locke was in a unique position to address the acquisition of land in the new English colonies in America. He was appointed secretary to the Lords Proprietors of Carolina in 1668, during which time debates raged as to the efficacy of plantations and their contribution to England's food security and economy in the aftermath of the Glorious Revolution. Locke was greatly influenced by the leading authorities of the day who favoured plantation agriculture.[13] The language of improvement thus accompanied the justification for settlement and development of agricultural land in Locke's work. These early colonies were treated very much as appendages to England: references to socage in the land grants of the New World were derived from the English tenurial system, the law thus making no distinction between heath and prairie.[14] America had been integrated into the unitary space of the British Empire,[15] its land use no longer reflecting the capabilities or limits of its ecosystems and peoples, but the demands of the English economy.

This idea of vacant space was enabled by Locke's dismissal of Native land use, so 'primitive' in impact that nature remained virtually unspoiled in the Americas. Locke never contemplated land uses that did not correspond to legally defined property, as his theory depended on the nature/culture dichotomy of propertied, civilised communities versus uncivilised communities on open land. He thus conflated the commons with open access resources, which meant that Native Americans were 'disqualified...as proprietors'.[16] There was already precedent for this type of treatment of open land in the form of English enclosure. This practice was extended to the New World and

---

[11] Ibid 47.

[12] Locke, *TT* Book II 137: As Much Land as a Man Tills, Plants, Improves, Cultivates, and can use the Product of, so much is his Property. He by his Labour does, as it were, inclose it from the Common. See also Barbara Arneil, 'Trade, Plantations, and Property: John Locke and the Economic Defense of Colonialism' (1994) *Journal of the History of Ideas* 55(4): 591–609, 602; Graham 55.

[13] Arneil 597.

[14] The Second Charter of Virginia; May 23, 1609, The Avalon Project, http://avalon.law.yale.edu/17th_century/va02.asp accessed 5 October 2020.

[15] Arneil 600.

[16] Allan Greer, 'Commons and Enclosure in the Colonization of North America' (2012) *The American Historical Review* 117(2): 365–386, 368.

can therefore be applied to Indigenous peoples evicted from their communal territories and homelands.[17]

Historically, enclosure, or the gradual ending of open-field farming in England and Wales, was accomplished through the fencing, parcelling and titling of these communal spaces.[18] Displaced commoners were rarely compensated; their villages were dismantled, so they subsequently sought labour in rapidly industrialising urban centres, succumbed to 'vagrancy' or were transported to the colonies. As common lands were consolidated for commercial ventures as well as luxury estate parks, the landed class expanded in wealth and power, a reflection of the rise of agrarian and later industrial capitalism.

In delineating property rights, Locke envisaged such common land as waste, disregarding its original meaning. Collectively owned land in the surrounding area beyond local croplands (be it moor, mountain, marsh or forest) was called 'the waste' in England, and it was multifunctional: it served as rough pasture for livestock, or a source for firewood or peat for fuel, provided herbs for local medicine, rushes for basketry or thatching, timber for construction and so on.[19] Waste was subject to a plethora of rules and customs governing access to these resources, often locally, regionally or nationally derived given the quality or significance of the resource. Locke dismissed these complex and creative land management practices and uses associated with waste. Waste was redefined as idle land, land in its primitive, uncultivated, underutilised state and the (global) commons. Locke himself describes, 'land that is left wholly to nature, that has no improvement of pasturage, tillage, or planting, is called, as indeed it is, waste; and we shall find the benefit of it amount to little more than nothing.[20]

In fact, waste is conflated with common land:

> To which let me add, that he who appropriates land to himself by his labor, does not lessen, but increases the common stock of mankind: for the provisions serving to the support of human life, produced by one acre of enclosed and cultivated land, are (to speak much within compass) ten times more than those which are yielded by an acre of land of an equal richness lying *waste in common*.[21]

Given this background, enclosure is therefore necessary and positive:

---

[17] Kenneth Olwig refers to this as 'virtual' enclosure' the spatial consolidation of land, reducing its biodiversity and land uses. See Olwig, 'Virtual Enclosure' 253.

[18] Charles Geisler, 'Disowned by the Ownership Society: How Native Americans Lost Their Land' (2014) *Rural Sociology* 79(1): 56–78. https://doi.org/10.1111/ruso.12028.

[19] Greer 369.

[20] Locke, *TT* Book II, 143.

[21] Ibid 140 (emphasis added).

And therefore he that encloses land, and has a greater plenty of the conveniences of life from ten acres, than he could have from a hundred left to nature, may truly be said to give ninety acres to mankind: for his labor now supplies him with provisions out of ten acres, which were but the product of a hundred lying in common.[22]

The implication is that, God gives man land in common, as uncultivated nature.[23] Superior usage of land is generated when man removes it from the common state through his labour.[24] Locke understood that commons were managed and worked by communities and provided the foundations of the peasant economy in England. This included other values, social, cultural and ecological, but Locke would not accord these any priority. Dowling notes that while a Lockean approach to land could conceive of 'sentimental' attachments, land's primary value is its exchange value: the possibility of producing value for use in exchange.[25] Locke deemed it naturally unjust for one to amass too much land; thus, the real source of wealth derived from land is the owner's opportunity to exchange the perishable items land produces for more durable forms of wealth, such as money.[26] Where land is located therefore does not matter, once it supplies this value. Such uncultivated and passive nature could be transposed anywhere, even to America, home of Locke's 'wild Indian', and easily recognised as abhorrent to Locke given the squandered potential for generating wealth:

> The fruit, or venison, which nourishes the wild Indian, *who knows no enclosure, and is still a tenant in common*, must be his, and so his, i.e. a part of him, that another can no longer have any right to it, before it can do him any good for the support of his life.[27]

Locke links together in consistently negative contexts the words 'commons', 'waste', 'commoner', 'Indian', 'America' and 'poverty'.[28] But

---

[22] Ibid.

[23] Locke, *TT* Book II, 134: And nobody has originally a private dominion, exclusive of the rest of mankind, in any of them, as they are thus in their natural state: yet being given for the use of men, there must of necessity be a means to appropriate them some way or other, before they can be of any use, or at all beneficial to any particular man.

[24] Locke, *TT* Book II 135: It being by him removed from the common state nature has placed it in, it has by this labour something annexed to it, that excludes the common right of other men: for this labor being the unquestionable property of the labourer, no man but he can have a right to what that is once joined to, at least where there is enough, and as good, left in common for others.

[25] Dowling at fn 8.

[26] Dowling 917. See also Zev Trachtenberg, 'The Takings Clause and the Meanings of Land' in Andrew Light and Jonathan M. Smith (eds), *Space, Place and Environmental Ethics* (1997) 63, 73.

[27] Locke, *TT* Book II 134, emphasis added.

[28] Greer 367.

Allan Greer highlights that the commons might be thought of both as a place—the village pasture—and as a set of access rights, such as grazing; in America, this portion of the commons located in the tillage zone of a given community might be designated the 'inner commons', interacting with the outer commons or outer zone beyond the village where local people gathered firewood, wild herbs and berries and other resources.[29] Greer notes that this was not the universal commons, but rather territory and resources that belonged to a particular person, lineage or community, roughly analogous to the moors, mountains and forests of Europe: common property, but neither unregulated nor open to everyone.[30]

Locke's application of the 'wild Indian' stereotype fails to address the reality of Native land use and conceptualisations of property in pre-Columbian America. Native Americans were hunter-gatherers, as well as dedicated farmers living in diverse environments across the continent.[31] Because land was not a commodity as Locke defined it, but the bulwark of Indian identity, exchanging it for currency was antithetical to their way of life.[32] Greer observes that landholding and land interests across pre-Columbian America varied from one environmental setting and subsistence regime to the next, shaped in some areas by legal codes and customs, as well as by the factors cited by Locke: population density, government and commerce.[33]

Agriculture in pre-Columbian America was primarily crop-based, and in the literal sense, land was not enclosed because animal husbandry was limited.[34] However, land was managed, as individual families or lineages did have particular plots of their own, subject to varying degrees of community control. Within cities lay villages with intensively cultivated fields reflecting a spectrum of interests: they could be owned by particular households, temples, local chiefs or a particular class of urban nobles and worked by the community.[35] Hunter-gatherer tenure developed according to function, such as hunting, fishing and berrying, which in turn shaped the way space was understood and defined.[36] Various groups lay claim to overlapping areas for distinct foraging purposes, depending on the resource or the ecosystem. The same may be said for shared waterways. It was possible for people of different nations to share hunting grounds; however, outsiders who hunted without authorisation could

[29] Ibid 369.
[30] Greer 370.
[31] Geisler 59.
[32] Ibid 61.
[33] Greer 369.
[34] Ibid.
[35] Ibid.
[36] Ibid 371.

be subject to violent punitive action.[37] This indicates that various Indigenous peoples were not passive actors, but managed and manipulated their environments through a wide variety of land use arrangements (privately or communally owned, collectively managed) subject to a range of use rights.[38]

The law in colonial America nevertheless relies on the passive, primitive Indian stereotype in relation to land use. It has been suggested that Native Americans willingly sold land, and evidence of market transfers challenges the conquest narrative of the New World, since Europeans bought rather than seized land.[39] However, the loss of land through market mechanisms does not mean that legal land transfers were not coercive, given that Native Americans were not recognised as capable of owning the land they were supposed to be freely selling.[40] Legislation was passed to this effect, relying on 'benevolent government stewardship' to facilitate land transfers that ultimately dispossessed Native peoples of their land, though this was deemed impartial where the letter of the law was concerned.[41]

As Arneil notes, Locke's claim that the state of nature could still be found in America was reinforced by his deliberate and repeated use of America and its natives in his property chapter.[42] Native landscapes thus played an important role in the development of Locke's theory of property, as their enclosure enabled the 'property as individual ownership' model to flourish. Locke removes the locally distinct character of landscapes and highlights instead the distinctiveness of the rational individual in withdrawing land from the homogenous uncivilised wilderness, adding value through labour to create private property. This theory relies on an uncultivated nature that is open access, in order to emphasise the role of the individual, at the expense of landscape.

The notion of a universal commons completely open to all—Locke's 'America'—existed mainly in the imperial imagination. To this pre-owned continent came Spanish, English and French colonists, occupying space, appropriating resources, and developing tenure practices to suit their purposes.[43] Native peoples were dispossessed in a variety of ways, as settlers claimed land as individual families or as a community sharing resources; these practices excluded

---

[37] Ibid.

[38] Ibid 372.

[39] Geisler 58.

[40] Ibid.

[41] Geisler 61: A series of Non-Intercourse Acts between 1790 and 1834 disallowed land conveyances between Indians and non-Indians if not sanctioned by the federal government. Enclosure became official federal policy during the Andrew Jackson presidency, beginning with forced removal of Native peoples from the Southeastern United States to the West.

[42] Arneil notes that of the 22 references listed by Peter Laslett concerning America or Indians, 10 occur in the 26 paragraphs of the chapter on property—see Arneil 67.

[43] Greer 372.

Native peoples, changing the landscape and affecting their livelihoods.[44] John Locke's misdescription of colonial property formation as the enclosure of a great universal commons served both to erase Native property in land at the outset and associate colonial appropriation with 'improvement', the latter to be understood both in its specialised agricultural sense and its more general meaning.[45] Diverse working Native landscapes became open-access resources, to be absorbed by European settler interests to secure economic development.

Locke's theories about property facilitated the appropriation and consolidation of land in the New World. As Indigenous legal scholars have observed, abstract private property rights imposed a culturally exclusive vision of land that aligned with post-medieval England, and was completely alien to pre-Columbian America.[46] This severed the relationship between local Indigenous use of the natural environment and democratic institutions, and the loss of local knowledge and expertise resulted in the absence of Indigenous contributions to the formation of environmentally and socially benign land governance.[47] The law's spatial severance of North America's pre-existing ecosystems and societies continues to inform the American legal system and fails to safeguard Indigenous interests today.[48]

As Roxanne Dunbar-Ortiz writes:

> ... [H]ad North America been a wilderness, undeveloped, without roads, and uncultivated, it might still be so, for the European colonists could not have survived. They appropriated what had already been created by Indigenous civilizations. They stole already cultivated farmland and the corn, vegetables, tobacco, and other crops domesticated over centuries, took control of the deer parks that had been cleared and maintained by Indigenous communities, used existing roads and water routes in order to move armies to conquer, and relied on captured Indigenous people to identify the locations of water, oyster beds, and medicinal herbs.[49]

---

[44] Ibid 372, and at 379.

[45] Ibid 385.

[46] John Borrows, 'Living Between Water and Rocks: First Nations, Environmental Planning and Democracy' (1997) *University of Toronto Law Journal* 47(4): 417–468, 431. For the Australian Aboriginal context, see Aileen Moreton-Robinson, *The White Possessive: Property, Power, and Indigenous Sovereignty* (University of Minnesota Press 2015); Irene Watson, *Aboriginal Peoples, Colonialism and International Law: Raw Law* (Routledge, Abingdon, 2015).

[47] Borrows 431.

[48] Attention has been called to the importance of these ancient practices as they find expression in modern Native communities today, which could be relevant for contemporary land claims and resource use rights. See Victor Thompson and others, 'The Early Materialization of Democratic Institutions among the Ancestral Muskogean of the American Southeast' (2022) *American Antiquity* 1: 704–723.

[49] Dunbar-Ortiz, *An Indigenous Peoples' History of the United States* (Beacon Press 2014) 46.

In this useful catalogue of the various interests and relations Indigenous peoples had developed with land, it is clear why landscapes had to be collapsed in order to recreate property. The interchangeable commons, vacuous space or wilderness, was the raw material to be mixed with labour, the clay of property, and the primitive 'Indian', at one with nature, was therefore unpropertised. The common law recognises those who would separate property from 'the great commons of unowned things'[50] and Locke's association of common land with open-access resources, and conflation of waste with idleness, lay the groundwork for advancing an individual's private property rights in land in Anglo-American land law.

REFERENCES

B Arneil, 'Trade, Plantations, and Property: John Locke and the Economic Defense of Colonialism' (1994) *Journal of the History of Ideas* 55(4): 591–609.

J Borrows, 'Living Between Water and Rocks: First Nations, Environmental Planning and Democracy' (1997) *University of Toronto Law Journal* 47(4): 417–468.

A Clarke, *Principles of Property Law* (Cambridge University Press 2020).

AC Dowling, 'Un-Locke-ing a Just Right Environmental Regime: Overcoming the Three Bears of International Environmentalism—Sovereignty, Locke, and Compensation' (2002) *William & Mary Environmental Law and Policy Review* 26: 891–960.

R Dunbar-Ortiz, *An Indigenous Peoples' History of the United States* (Beacon Press 2014).

C Geisler, 'Disowned by the Ownership Society: How Native Americans Lost Their Land' (2014) *Rural Sociology* 79(1): 56–78.

N Graham, *Lawscape: Property, Environment, Law* (Routledge-Cavendish 2010).

A Greer, 'Commons and Enclosure in the Colonization of North America' (2012) *The American Historical Review* 117(2): 365–386.

J Locke *Two Treatises of Government* (first published 1689, Hackett Publishing Company 2016).

A Moreton-Robinson, *The White Possessive: Property, Power, and Indigenous Sovereignty* (University of Minnesota Press 2015).

K Olwig 'Virtual Enclosure, Ecosystem Services, Landscape's Character and the 'Rewilding' of the Commons: The 'Lake District' Case' (2016) *Landscape Research* 41(2): 253–264.

C Rose, 'Possession as the Origin of Property' (1985) *The University of Chicago Law Review* 52(1): 73–86.

VD Thompson, J Holland-Lulewicz, RA Butler, TW Hunt, L Wendt, J Wettstaed, M Williams et al, 'The Early Materialization of Democratic Institutions among the Ancestral Muskogean of the American Southeast' (2022) *American Antiquity* 87(1): 704–723.

Z Trachtenberg, 'The Takings Clause and the Meanings of Land' in Andrew Light and Jonathan M. Smith (eds), *Space, Place and Environmental Ethics* (Rowman & Littlefield 1997).

---

[50] Carol Rose, 'Possession as the Origin of Property' (1985) *The University of Chicago Law Review* 52(1): 73–86, 88.

J Waldron, *The Right to Private Property* (Clarendon Press 1988).
I Watson, *Aboriginal Peoples, Colonialism and International Law: Raw Law* (Routledge, Abingdon 2015).

Open Access This chapter is licensed under the terms of the Creative Commons Attribution 4.0 International License (http://creativecommons.org/licenses/by/4.0/), which permits use, sharing, adaptation, distribution and reproduction in any medium or format, as long as you give appropriate credit to the original author(s) and the source, provide a link to the Creative Commons license and indicate if changes were made.

The images or other third party material in this chapter are included in the chapter's Creative Commons license, unless indicated otherwise in a credit line to the material. If material is not included in the chapter's Creative Commons license and your intended use is not permitted by statutory regulation or exceeds the permitted use, you will need to obtain permission directly from the copyright holder.

CHAPTER 4

Blackstone and the Externalisation of Landscape

Abstract The idea of absolutist ownership in land, introduced in William Blackstone's influential work, *Commentaries on the Laws of England*, is the subject of this chapter. Blackstone's reframing of intrinsic aspects of the landscape as external encumbrances burdening the individual landowner is discussed as the watershed moment that terminated property's social function. Blackstone applied the generic feudal pyramid of tenures to England, without considering the lived-in experiences of local communities and their ancient way of life that varied and complicated feudal practices. The chapter examines the role of the new landowning class in Parliament, which passed the Enclosure Acts to enclose common land as private property, thereby using the law to dismantle common rights and functioning local communities, and legitimise exclusion as a feature of property.

Keywords Blackstone · Exclusion · Absolutist model · Tenures · Feudal pyramid · Commons · Enclosure Acts

While Locke's labour theory of value provided the pretext for acquiring property by separating it from common land, Sir William Blackstone emphasised the exclusionary character of property, in which rights are consolidated in a single landowner, to the exclusion of all others.[1] This expression of the

---

[1] Clarke, 'Principles of Property' 185; Jane B Baron, 'Rescuing the Bundle-of-Rights Metaphor in Property Law' (2013) *University of Cincinnati Law Review* 82: 57–102.

ideology of exclusion[2] has remained the defining feature of Blackstonian property for about 250 years, though it has since been modified.[3] It is best captured in Blackstone's oft-quoted passage in the 'Commentaries on the Laws of England'[4]:

> There is nothing which so generally strikes the imagination, and engages the affections of mankind, as the right of property; or that sole and despotic dominion which one man claims and exercises over the external things of the world, in total exclusion of the right of any other individual in the universe.[5]

Although it is questionable whether Blackstone himself believed in property as an absolute right to exclude,[6] the Blackstonian conception is entrenched as the dominant Western property ideology, inclusive of civil law jurisdictions.[7] What is relevant is that the right to exclude means that one has property; conversely, to the extent that one does not have exclusion rights, one does not have property.[8] In this definition, property is so absolute as to permit no infringement, not even for the common good.[9] According to Blackstone, absolute rights are those rights that every man is entitled to enjoy, not because of his membership in society, but by virtue of his individuality.[10] Property was an absolute right vested in the individual by the immutable law of nature, independent of societal recognition.[11] Private property was a key development in mankind's advancement, as individuals emerged from the global commons to establish themselves in permanent homes and grow crops. Occupancy or use rights thus ripened into permanent and exclusive dominion over the thing—private property.[12] It was only in very limited circumstances that society

---

[2] Benjamin Davy, '"Dehumanized Housing" and the Ideology of Property as a Social Function' (2020) *Planning Theory* 19(1): 38–58, 38; Thomas W Merrill, 'Property and the Right to Exclude' (1998) *Nebraska Law Review* 77: 730–755, 734.

[3] Clarke 186.

[4] William Blackstone, *Commentaries on the Laws of England* (hereafter cited as Bl Comm.) (Oxford 1765–1769).

[5] 2 Bl Comm 2.

[6] David B. Schorr, 'How Blackstone Became a Blackstonian' (2009) *Theoretical Inquiries in Law* 10: 103–126, 104; Albert W. Alschuler, 'Rediscovering Blackstone' (1996) *University of Pennsylvania Law Review* 45(1): 1–56; Carol M. Rose, 'Canons of Property Talk, or, Blackstone's Anxiety' (1998) *Yale Law Journal* 108: 601–633.

[7] See, for example, Article 544 of the Code Napoléon. Davy 41.

[8] Merrill 753.

[9] Vandevelde 332.

[10] 1 Bl Comm 122–124.

[11] Robert P. Burns, 'Blackstone's Theory of the Absolute Rights of Property' (1985) *University of Cincinnati Law Review* 54: 67–87.

[12] Burns 75; Alschuler 32.

could constrain this right in order to promote other objectives.[13] Blackstone underscores the primacy of the individual right of property by stating that:

> So great moreover is the regard of the law for private property, that it will not authorize the least violation of it; no, not even for the general good of the whole community. If a new road, for instance, were to be made through the grounds of a private person, it might perhaps be extensively beneficial to the public; but the law permits no man, or set of men to do this without consent of the owner of the land.[14]

Blackstone therefore privileges ownership above other interests in land. In spite of the recognition of those interests, it is in very rare circumstances that private property can be imposed upon and Parliament will restrict property rights to promote the public good.[15] In such a case, Parliament can 'oblige the owner to alienate his possessions for a reasonable price; and even this is an exertion of powers, which the legislature indulges with caution, and which nothing but the legislature can perform'.[16] As an ardent supporter of Parliament,[17] Blackstone was very concerned with the arbitrary and corrupt use of this Parliamentary power to deprive landowners of their land, and noted such decisions would not be binding.[18]

There were particular reasons for this stance. At the time of Blackstone's writing, the legislature comprised landed members who had benefited from the agricultural revolution, and specifically enacted laws to deprive commoners of their land; it is unlikely that they would have tolerated any encroachment on their newly enclosed lands, and therefore, to oppose enclosure, especially after 1730, was illegal.[19] The intersection of land ownership with law-making powers[20] in Blackstone's day thus cannot be overlooked when considering his explication of the foundations of private property, and provides context for his defence of landowners.

Blackstone was determined to secure the common law's position as the law of the English and contrasted what he deemed 'foreign' Norman law with the endogenous common law. To emphasise the 'oppressiveness' of Norman law, he focused on the body of law it had displaced, Saxon law and its perceived

---

[13] Alschuler 34.
[14] 1 Bl Comm 139.
[15] Alschuler 4.
[16] 1 Bl Comm 139.
[17] Dennis R Nolan, 'Sir William Blackstone and the New American Republic: A Study of Intellectual Impact' (1976) *New York University Law Review* 51: 731–768, 735.
[18] Alschuler 30.
[19] Graham 71.
[20] Ibid.

individual freedoms.[21] Embedding this view involved recasting the lived-in values and experiences of commoners in the landscape as constraints upon the land, introduced through the Norman feudal system of tenure.[22] By the eighteenth century, the various lay tenures could be reduced to two kinds: the free tenure in common (socage) and the base tenure by a copy of court roll.[23] Free socage lands were those held directly from the king, having supplanted a previously complex system of military tenures.[24] Blackstone discussed the etymology of 'socage', which he chose to derive from 'soc', a Saxon word signifying 'liberty' or 'privilege'. He favoured this definition to that of the common lawyers, who generally derived it from the Latin soca meaning 'plough', thereby connecting the tenure with services of husbandry. Blackstone concluded that the socage tenures were the relics of Saxon liberty,[25] as there had been no pre-existing Saxon feudal law.[26]

While free socage tenure was conditioned upon rendering services to the king, copyhold tenure was conditioned upon the will of the lord.[27] The copyholder in Blackstone's day could however not be deprived of his tenure arbitrarily. Rather, his rights were 'fixed and ascertained by the custom to be the same and no other, that has time out of mind been exercised and declared by his ancestors'.[28] The freehold remained solely in the lord, 'who hath granted out the use and occupation, but not the corporal seisin or true legal possession, of certain parcels thereof, to these his customary tenants at will'.[29] This provided Blackstone the pretext for stripping away the social dimensions of landscape, by re-envisaging non-ownership interests as burdens on the land.

To emphasise the imposition of these 'feudal incidents', Blackstone describes a feudal pyramid of obligations that relies on problematic historic sources from English medieval property law, complicating the identification and classification of property as it relates to land. As Susan Reynolds notes, 'tenure' is an anachronistic and misleading term to apply to medieval English property, because it arose from doubtful translations and misunderstandings of medieval law that originated in the seventeenth century.[30] The 'feudal tenure' of Anglophone historians is a blend of scholars' interpretation of

---

[21] 2 Bl Comm 51–52; John Cairns, 'Blackstone, the Ancient Constitution and the Feudal Law' (1985) *The Historical Journal* 28(3): 711–717, 717.

[22] Burns 79.

[23] 2 Bl Comm 101.

[24] Ibid 78–81; Burns 80.

[25] Cairns 716; 2 Bl Comm 81.

[26] Cairns 715.

[27] 2 Bl Comm 147.

[28] Ibid.

[29] Ibid 148.

[30] Susan Reynolds, 'Tenure and Property in Medieval England' (2015) *Historical Research* 88(242): 563–576, 563.

Thomas Littleton's fifteenth-century Tenures, with sixteenth-century French scholars' version of late medieval academic law that they had derived from the Consuetudines Feudorum or Libri Feudorum, compiled in twelfth-century Italy.[31]

Blackstone elevated his theory to a doctrine of tenures, meaning that 'all the land in the kingdom is supposed to be holden, mediately or immediately, of the king.'[32] But the Normans were concerned with administration and revenue-raising, rather than immediately imposing a system of law—it would have been easier to add to the pre-existing obligations of property-holders than to diminish their traditional rights. Special emergencies may have required special demands that eventually mellowed into custom—in the aftermath of the conquest, military service was probably an immediate priority, followed by other 'feudal incidents'. Land being subject to royal jurisdiction did not necessarily indicate subordination or less than normal free rights of property, and yet, tenure was generally applied to all forms of medieval English property, without a full analysis of its rights and obligations.[33]

This conflation of property and jurisdiction as an essential characteristic of feudal law comes from historians rather than medieval law itself.[34] In fact, by the thirteenth century, the hierarchy of military service and 'incidents' appeared more as a social hierarchy of different kinds of property than the hierarchy of jurisdiction and government that developed elsewhere. As the legal profession developed in thirteenth-century England, streamlined terminology fused Latin and French concepts—anyone who held land, with all its attendant rights and obligations, was correspondingly called a tenant, absent any of the connotations of fewer rights and more obligations that are implied in the modern use of the word, and probably due to consensus among judges and advocates.[35] Courts began to ignore the lower layers of rights that they had once accepted, so that they increasingly favoured lords of manors at the expense of copyholders.[36] In the sixteenth century, as a result of their reading, English historians and antiquaries now began to employ a new vocabulary that had not been current in English common law but rather had passed into professional French law from academic French works.[37]

English academics appeared to have treated French law works as merely recording the law as it developed, but the law of fiefs that originated in the Lombard Libri Feudorum was not analogous to English common law and the

---

[31] Reynolds 564.
[32] 2 Bl Comm 59.
[33] Reynolds 569–570.
[34] Ibid 567–568.
[35] Ibid 568.
[36] EP Thompson, *Customs in Common* (The New Press 1991) 114–164; AW Brian Simpson, *A History of the Land Law* (Clarendon Press 1986) 108; Reynolds 570.
[37] Reynolds 571.

local variation in customary law.[38] England's seemingly perfect feudal pyramid generated new layers of property rights, while in fact obscuring so many differences: the difference between customary law, professional law and academic law, as well as that between English common law and the professional law that developed across the channel.[39] Blackstone's reliance on these texts and their interpretations, combined with the Commentaries' accessible and elegant style, was responsible for this diffusion of the doctrine of tenure as the basis of English property law.[40]

The reality of the pre-enclosure commons overturns Blackstone's generic feudal pyramid. As Graham notes, the property relationship held especially by commoners pre-enclosure was closer to the original sense of the word property, referring to identification with and from place, rather than ownership over it.[41] Place specificity generated a subjective relationship that bound commoners in a mutually dependent relationship with the land; as members of a peasant economy based on open-field agriculture, they shared a heritage and identity and so land was not alienable or exclusive because its value was not purely economic.[42] That shared heritage reflected continuity with the past, and was derived from generations of occupancy, or the habitus of landscape, articulated and reinforced in the laws and rights of the commons.[43]

The original land laws of peasant economy were diverse rather than uniform; customs were locally developed, and relevant because they were sensitive to varying local geographic conditions.[44] Providing highly specific limits or conditions to rights of access, use and enjoyment of land and other local resources had been an early form of natural resource management, observed over centuries.[45] The pre-enclosure local representative councils, and the corpus of customary law they established, shaped the land, thereby forming a 'substantive landscape' or polity, in the legal sense of 'creating and defining rights and duties'.[46] Customary law was thus the formalisation and ritualisation of habits and practices, reinterpreted as required over time, and forming a bank of cultural memory and common identity.[47]

---

[38] Ibid 575.

[39] Ibid 576.

[40] Reynolds notes that 50 years after the Law of Property Act, law students were still taught that a feudal structure had been imposed in England during the Norman conquest, with the king at the apex and land held either 'directly of the King' or 'of' others under him. See Reynolds 574.

[41] Graham 74–75.

[42] JM Neeson, *Commoners: Common Right, Enclosure and Social Change in England, 1700–1820* (Cambridge University Press 1993) 321 and 3–5.

[43] Neeson 297–298.

[44] Graham 53.

[45] Ibid.

[46] Olwig, 'Virtual Enclosure' 256.

[47] Olwig, *Landscape, Nature and the Body Politic* 58 and at 60.

In Blackstone's time, the suppression of these customary rights of common people through the Enclosure Acts was not the result of an intrinsic failure of land management methods, or diminishing fertility of these lands, or even the collapse of these communities, but simply because the land could be acquired for 'improvement,'[48] which enriched the landed class.[49] Enclosure occurred regardless of the location of these lands, and the law minimised the extent of common rights in order to limit compensation due to commoners.[50] Common rights have never recovered their depth and complexity since. Private property was thus not the inevitable outcome of a linear process in which a progressive society eventually replaced an inefficient common property model; it was a deliberate policy choice that ignored extant cultural perspectives on land and eliminated institutions for managing land efficiently as the basis of community life.

As David Tabachnick observes, 'the enclosing of the commons in England was not merely a physical process of putting up fences but also a conceptual process that created a new legal, economic, and sociological reality'. Blackstone was the foremost contributor to this new legal reality. By importing French sources, rather than examining the lived in experiences of English commoners, who for centuries had interacted with Saxon then Norman systems, adapting to maintain their communities, Blackstone presented a model of property that was clear and simple, but ahistoric and aspatial. In order to do so, Blackstone developed a history of land law that freed the landowner from the 'weight' of myriad obligations that had characterised land during the feudal period. Now, ownership is absolutist, with the ability to exclude, making inhabitants foreigners in their own community, without representation and their way of life undesirable and even lawless.

Through this filter of hyper-individuality, ancient communal rights and practices that had arisen during the Anglo-Saxon and later Norman periods,

---

[48] Tabachnick notes that Lord Longborough, who ruled in the Houghton case upholding Lord Cornwallis' right to enclose lands and extinguish common property rights, was a devotee of improvement theory and mischaracterised common property, in this case, the limited and communally regulated right of parish members to glean, as unregulated open access, or as he says, 'universal promiscuous enjoyment'. In this way, he could strip away common rights overlapping private ownership, which had since time immemorial defined English property in land. See Tabachnick 497–498 and Steel v Houghton 1 BHH 51, 126 ER 32.

[49] Graham 54. Tabachnick 499: The destruction of common rights involved the destruction of the regulatory rules and democratic rule-making process of the manorial courts or village meetings that played the role of manorial courts where several manors existed in one parish. See also Neeson 111, footnote 2.

[50] The common law, over time, restricted recognition at common law of customary rights to very specific rights in land. According to the ruling in Gateward's Case, 6 Co. Rep. 59b, 60b, 77 Eng. Rep. 344, 345 (K.B. 1607), when land was enclosed, only those cotters who could present documentary evidence of their common rights, as opposed to those with unwritten customary rights, had a right to be consulted and to refuse consent, and only the former could get compensation for the loss of common rights. See Tabachnick 497.

enabling peasants and commoners to become self-sufficient and independent were now interpreted as dependence on the landowner's goodwill.[51] Protecting individual landowners' rights as justification for enclosure destroyed community governance of land, and with it, alternative perspectives that had defined the landscape. Stressing legal personal ownership placed the focus on acquisition rather than community approval in the use and management of land.[52] Property was no longer linked to landscape but required by definition to exclude the social elements of the landscape in the name of liberty. Though Saxon conceptualisations of land as earlier noted are cognate to the landscape, Blackstone interpreted Saxon liberty as an individual quality, not in terms of self-sufficiency for communities.

Blackstone's focus on individual ownership inverted property, from its associations with mutuality to one that was freed from social obligations to land—Blackstone does not expect landowners to fulfil a duty prior to confirming their 'sole and despotic dominion'.[53] He externalised the landscape by treating non-ownership interests as burdens, embellishments and even privileges awarded at the landowner's discretion. Ownership was therefore hierarchised in a way it had never been before. Excluding these connections with the land erased its distinctiveness, since the location, features and limits of the land would no longer define relations with it. Where communal uses were allowed, this was a concession on the part of the private property owner, not a right exercised by communities based on their mutual relationship with the landscape.

Blackstone's idealised tenurial system served to mask the complex cultural perspectives towards land following the conquest. For Blackstone, ownership, previously non-exclusionary and qualified by a range of interests, became absolute. This anti-social conceptualisation of land would have sounded the death knell for landscape, by eliminating communal land values from property. This has contributed to property's current paradoxical character as an anti-social institution that nevertheless structures human relationships in society.[54] Although Blackstone associated property with things, the predominant character of ownership enabled the abstraction of the concept. Bentham, Blackstone's former student and among his fiercest critics, eliminates land altogether in his positivisation of property theory. By the beginning of the twentieth century, the Blackstonian conception of property had been replaced by Wesley Newcomb Hohfeld's dephysicalised property model, in which property was defined by abstract relations between people, rather than a tangible

---

[51] Jesse Goldstein, 'Terra Economica: Waste and the Production of Enclosed Nature' (2012) *Antipode* 45(2): 357–375, 371.

[52] Deller 151.

[53] Davy 52.

[54] Joseph William Singer and Jack M. Beermann 'The Social Origins of property' (July 1993) *Canadian Journal of Law and Jurisprudence* VI(2): 217–248, 228.

object.[55] Property law, therefore, continued to diverge from place-determined ideas about land in the development of the common law.

REFERENCES

AW Alschuler, 'Rediscovering Blackstone' (1996) *University of Pennsylvania Law Review* 45(1): 1–56.
JB Baron, 'Rescuing the Bundle-of-Rights Metaphor in Property Law' (2013) *University of Cincinnati Law Review* 82: 57–102.
W Blackstone, *Commentaries on the Laws of England* (Oxford 1765–1769).
RP Burns, 'Blackstone's Theory of the Absolute Rights of Property' (1985) *University of Cinncinati Law Review* 54: 67–87.
J Cairns, 'Blackstone, the Ancient Constitution and the Feudal Law' (1985) *The Historical Journal* 28(3): 711–717.
A Clarke, *Principles of Property Law* (Cambridge University Press 2020).
B Davy '"Dehumanized Housing" and the Ideology of Property as a Social Function' (2020) *Planning Theory* 19(1): 38–58.
W Deller 'The Transfer of Land in Medieval England from 1246 to 1430: The Language of Acquisition' (2020) *Continuity and Change* 35: 139–162.
J Goldstein, 'Terra Economica: Waste and the Production of Enclosed Nature' (2012) *Antipode* 45(2): 357–375.
N Graham, *Lawscape: Property, Environment, Law* (Routledge-Cavendish 2010).
TW Merrill 'Property and the Right to Exclude' (1998) *Nebraska Law Review* 77: 730–755.
JM Neeson, *Commoners: Common Right, Enclosure and Social Change in England, 1700–1820* (Cambridge University Press 1993).
DR Nolan, 'Sir William Blackstone and the New American Republic: A Study of Intellectual Impact' (1976) *New York University Law Review* 51: 731–768.
K Olwig, *Landscape, Nature and the Body Politic: From Britain's Renaissance to America's New World* (University of Wisconsin Press 2002).
———, 'Virtual Enclosure, Ecosystem Services, Landscape's Character and the "Rewilding" of the Commons: The "Lake District" Case' (2016) *Landscape Research* 41(2): 253–264.
S Reynolds, 'Tenure and Property in Medieval England' (2015) *Historical Research* 88(242): 563–576.
CM Rose, 'Canons of Property Talk, or, Blackstone's Anxiety' (1998) *The Yale Law Journal* 108: 601–633.
DB Schorr, 'How Blackstone Became a Blackstonian' (2009) *Theoretical Inquiries in Law* 10: 103–126.
AWB Simpson, *A History of the Land Law* (Clarendon Press 1986).
JW Singer and JM Beermann 'The Social Origins of Property' (July 1993) *Canadian Journal of Law and Jurisprudence* VI(2): 217–248.
D Tabachnick, 'Two Models of Ownership: How Commons Has Co-Existed with Private Property' (2016) *American Journal of Economics and Sociology* 75(2): 488–563.
EP Thompson, *Customs in Common* (The New Press 1991).

---

[55] Vandevelde, 330 and 360.

KJ Vandevelde, 'The New Property of the Nineteenth Century: The Development of the Modern Concept of Property' (1980) *Buffalo Law Review* 29: 325–368.

Open Access This chapter is licensed under the terms of the Creative Commons Attribution 4.0 International License (http://creativecommons.org/licenses/by/4.0/), which permits use, sharing, adaptation, distribution and reproduction in any medium or format, as long as you give appropriate credit to the original author(s) and the source, provide a link to the Creative Commons license and indicate if changes were made.

The images or other third party material in this chapter are included in the chapter's Creative Commons license, unless indicated otherwise in a credit line to the material. If material is not included in the chapter's Creative Commons license and your intended use is not permitted by statutory regulation or exceeds the permitted use, you will need to obtain permission directly from the copyright holder.

CHAPTER 5

Marx and the Dephysicalisation of the Landscape

Abstract This chapter relies on Marx's later critiques of capitalism (which focused on the relationship between property rights and nature) to explain the final hallmark of property: alienability. Using Marx's metabolic rift theory, the chapter considers how the abstraction of land was achieved through the separation of culture and nature, which created distance between people and their embedded relations with land. This is illustrated with examples from rundale communities in Ireland and the slave colonies of the Caribbean. Converting landscapes to plantation monoculture to maximise exploitation destabilised the landscape dynamic, facilitating displacement, oppression, and enslavement, and socio-ecological crises such as the Famine. The chapter thus draws attention to the spatial consequences of land's dephysicalisation in property law.

Keywords Metabolic rift · Capitalism · Alienation · Rundale · Slavery · Plantation · Ireland · Caribbean

The conceptual shift towards dephysicalised property as connectivity with land was lost forms part of Karl Marx's critique of capitalism. Marx's analysis of the negative impact of property rights on human communities through the rise of capitalism is contained in his major unfinished work Capital.[1] Saito notes that Marx's critique of capitalism became increasingly ecological as he emphasised the fundamental contradiction of capitalism—that its profitability relied on the

---

[1] K Marx, *Capital* (vol. 1, Penguin 1976).

destruction of the source of its wealth (natural resources).[2] This is achieved through the disruption of the link between man and nature, or metabolic rift, explained thus:

> Capitalist production... disturbs the metabolic interaction between man and the earth... All progress in capitalist agriculture is a progress in the art, not only of robbing the worker, but of robbing the soil; all progress in increasing the fertility of the soil for a given time is progress towards ruining the more long-lasting sources of that fertility... Capitalist production, therefore, only develops the technique and the degree of combination of the social process of production by simultaneously undermining the original sources of all wealth—the soil and the worker.[3]

The idea of an unalienated relationship between people and nature thus underscores Marx's philosophy of property and critique of capitalism.[4] A lived-in nature aligns with the landscape, though Marx never used this term and his work predates cultural geography. He did however see man as part of nature.[5] Alienation was originally defined as alienation from community, and Marx deployed the concept in the sense of the effect of estrangement of humanity from their existence within nature as a result of civilisation, or capitalist society.[6] Property was not land, but the ownership of it, and the alienable possession of land led to the 'objectifying, abstracting and then absenting of land'—alienation's dual nature meant it was both estrangement from land/nature and from other people.[7] Alienation according to Graham is a relationship that became positivised in the seventeenth and eighteenth centuries with the prevalence of absolute private property. Modern property law erases the bilateral aspect of alienation, constructing alienation as agency and will: the person is an active alienating subject, and the land, the passive alienated object of the land market.[8]

---

[2] Kohei Saito, 'Marx's Ecological Notebooks' (February 2016) *Monthly Review* 67(9): 25–42, 26.

[3] Marx, *Capital* (vol. 1) 637–638.

[4] K Marx, *The Marx Engels Reader* in R Tucker (ed) (New York: Norton 1978); Marx, *Early Writings* (Penguin 1992) 322. See also Graham 135; John Bellamy Foster and Brett Clark 'The Robbery of Nature: Capitalism and the Metabolic Rift' (July–August 2018) *Monthly Review* 1–20.

[5] K Marx, *Early Writings* 328: Man lives from nature, i.e. nature is his body, and he must maintain a continuing dialogue with it if he is not to die. To say that man's physical and mental life is linked to nature simply means that nature is linked to itself, for man is a part of nature.

[6] Graham 44.

[7] Ibid 45.

[8] Ibid.

For Marx, alienation is a result of the failure to recognise the human origin of objects produced by human activity, specifically their social origin, as products of co-operative social labour.[9] Marx observed that prior to capitalism, labour reflected the mutuality of social relations in a community attuned to nature, based on roles assigned within the peasant family unit.[10] When nature was valued solely through human labour and ownership, as a result of the transition to a capitalist economy, this extinguished the social relations of property.[11] Marx demonstrated his grasp of the significance of alienation when he articulated the full extent of the loss: the socio-cultural and environmental dimensions of property that once characterised the working landscape. Rendering land as abstract and alienable property therefore demanded the dephysicalisation of landscape, the separation of the socio-cultural (the communal bonds between people and the land) from the ecological, so that nature could be reduced to natural resources or raw material.

Marx thus described capitalism in terms of its capacity to destroy the ecosystem as well as human beings' relationships with nature. The capitalist economy failed to recognise the impact of its accumulation of capital on the underlying ecological conditions of human existence; these are mere side-effects, external social and environmental costs.[12] The alienation of labour under capitalism has as its precondition the alienation of nature—the severance of human beings from the land, and from their natural environment.[13] Labour, once a process between man and nature, became distorted in the capitalist commodity economy as the accumulation of capital is prioritised[14]: natural and human limits are exceeded, and human and social development ignored. There are numerous examples of the ecological devastation resulting

---

[9] S Vogel, 'Marx and Alienation from Nature' (1988) *Social Theory and Practice* 14(3): 367–387, 374.

[10] Marx, *Capital* (vol. 1) 171: The different kinds of labour ...such as tilling the fields, tending the cattle, spinning, weaving and making clothes—are already in their natural form social functions; for they are functions of the family, which, just as much as a society based on commodity production, possesses. its own spontaneously developed division of labour. The distribution of labour within the family and the labour-time expended by the individual members of the family, are regulated by differences of sex and age as well as by seasonal variations in the natural conditions of labour.

[11] Graham 46 and 152; Marx, *Capital* (vol. 1) 165–166: Objects of utility become commodities only because they are the products of the labour of private individuals who work independently of each other. ... Since the producers do not come into social contact until they exchange the products of their labour, the specific social characteristics of their private labours appear only within this exchange.... therefore, the social relations between their private labours appear as what they are, i.e. they do not appear as direct social relations between persons in their work, but rather as material relations between persons and social relations between things.

[12] John Bellamy Foster, 'The Rediscovery of Marx's Ecology' in Marcello Musto (ed), *The Marx Revival: Key Concepts and New Interpretations* (Cambridge 2020) 183.

[13] Bellamy Foster, 'Marx's Ecology' in *The Marx Revival* 185.

[14] Karl Marx, *Grundrisse* (London: Penguin 1973) 413.

from industrialised agriculture throughout the world,[15] and Marx discussed Ireland in this context.[16]

As described earlier, the rundale system of land tenure is associated with traditional land practices that predated the conquest of Ireland. Following the arrival of the English, land became increasingly unavailable to the general population as Ireland was rearranged into estates that operated on a commercial basis.[17] At the beginning of the nineteenth century, agriculture was characterised by extreme land subdivision and increasingly high rents, forcing traditional communities to relocate to the West of Ireland and adapt their land practices in order to survive in a harsher environment.[18] During this period, the potato was introduced, and while communities initially flourished, the dependence on this crop and monocultural practices must be understood in the wider context of British mercantile colonialism,[19] which expelled communities from their homes and set the stage for extinguishing communal bonds with land.[20]

Through the rundale system, peasant communities were able to fairly distribute land, while paying rents to their landlords.[21] Communal labour permeated all aspects of community life, and complex patterns of land use and distribution were preserved through lineage and kinship bonds, although these demonstrated flexibility as they were not exclusively patrilineal.[22] Availability of land shaped these practices and modifications were introduced over time. The functioning landscape relied on gavelkind or partible inheritance. Gavelkind meant that all members of the rundale community had a right to access the land, which could not be alienated. This communal property relationship ensured equality of access for all communal members. The amount of arable land held by an individual member under the rundale communal conditions was never quantified by units of measurement such as acres or furlongs, but by the potential ecological output (or value) of the land area

---

It is not the unity of living and active humanity with the natural, inorganic conditions of their metabolic exchange with nature...which requires explanation...but rather the separation between these inorganic conditions of human existence and this active existence, a separation which is completely posited only in the relation of wage labor and capital.

[15] Bellamy Foster, 'Marx's Ecology' in *The Marx Revival* 187.

[16] Marx, *Capital* (vol. 1) 860; Marx, 'Outline of a Report on the Irish Question to the Communist Educational Association of German Workers in London, December 16, 1867' in Marx and Engels (eds), *Ireland and the Irish Question* (Moscow 1978) 136-149; Eamonn Slater and Terrence McDonough, 'Marx on Nineteenth-Century Colonial Ireland: Analysing Colonialism as a Dynamic Social Process' (November 2008) *Irish Historical Studies* 36(142): 153-172, 172 and at 169.

[17] Braa 206 and discussed in Chapter 2.

[18] Ibid 207 and 194.

[19] Ibid 207.

[20] Graham 46 and 152.

[21] Braa 201, 198.

[22] Ibid 201-202.

and the sharing out of its ecological output equally among the communal members.[23] The tradition of communal co-operation characterised all activities in the rundale communities: crops were planted, tended and harvested by communal labour, as were herding and peat cutting.[24] The mechanism for maintaining these crucial activities and authority for regulating access relied on the recognition of various kinship bonds.

The introduction of the potato allowed for the concentration of the population, as the crop could be grown on a quarter of the land required for wheat.[25] The well-nourished population significantly expanded, but access to land did not under the British estate system. The fertility of potato crop yields on smaller and smaller plots of land enabled population growth and accelerated subdivision of land to support ever-increasing numbers of families, furthering dependence on the potato. This put pressure on the rundale system and the gavelkind mode of inheritance.[26]

Methods of destabilising connections to land were observable elsewhere in Ireland. Where other rundale systems were destroyed throughout Ireland to accommodate the creation of commercial estates, tenancy at will prevailed. This required peasants to bid against each other to obtain a lease, which drove up rents and created considerable land insecurity. Two forms of subtenancy, conacre and cottier, introduced peasant communities to wage–labour relations and cash cropping (markets). Cottier tenants agreed to pay a cash rent after a successful harvest of a key crop, such as wheat or oats, which was a means of increasing labour outputs into the production of food and cash crops, while conacre sublets supplemented cottier subtenancies, with more peasants and households subsisting on smaller plots of land.[27]

The intensification of these practices and the limiting of options for communities relying on the rundale system exhausted the soil, making these landscapes vulnerable to socio-ecological crises such as the Famine.[28] For Marx, the primary issue was not the plant pathogen itself, but the social conditions that had paved the way for the Famine, that is, the entire history of the rack-renting system and the subsequent transformation of the socio-ecological subsistence base of Ireland.[29] In impacting soil fertility, the social, economic and political integrity of land was undermined.[30] In monopolising access to

---

[23] Eamonn Slater and Eoin Flaherty, 'Marx on Primitive Communism: The Irish Rundale Agrarian Commune, Its Internal Dynamics and the Metabolic Rift' (2009) *Irish Journal of Anthropology* 12(2): 5–34, 12.

[24] Braa 202.

[25] Ibid 200.

[26] Ibid 203–204.

[27] Ibid 205–206.

[28] Bellamy Foster and Clark, *The Rift of Eire* 6.

[29] Ibid 7.

[30] Slater and McDonough 153.

land, landlords were able to exploit the Irish by 'rackrenting' them.[31] Both practices dismissed the natural limits of the land as communities had been undermined in their maintenance of these landscapes. Marx thus demonstrated that property rights could have implications for the physical limits of the environment.[32] This could not be separated from the social relations communities developed in their interaction with the environment.

The devastation that the Famine wrought can be traced to the artificially created dependence on the potato, a decision characteristic of a colonial land policy that prompted drastic changes to the landscape, substituting capitalistic modes of production that relied on monoculture and absorption of all cultivable land. Monoculture and the resultant Famine reflected particular understandings of land at odds with its natural limits and the communal bonds communities formed with the environment. The laissez faire approach to the economy promoted beliefs that the Famine was a natural phenomenon, and its adherents advocated a policy of non-intervention in order to allow for 'market adjustments'.[33] The practices and policies accompanying legal transfer of land in Ireland were thus never attuned to the rhythms of the landscape. Colonial land transfers were antithetical to the traditional way of life, and distorted the internal dynamic of the landscape that communities had relied upon for common survival. Ecosystems were pushed to their limits, as decisions were made that exhausted the soil, and communities were also destroyed through the pressures on communal land regimes, or dependence on land practices such as rack renting that were asynchronous with the local landscape.

Following the Famine, the loss of lives and high emigration facilitated the consolidation and commercialisation of land to reduce dependence on the potato.[34] Gavelkind gave way to primogeniture to avoid subdivision of holdings by partible inheritance, which also transformed kinship and marriage practices.[35] The Famine and industrialised agriculture eliminated the need for an institution to negotiate and divide lots in a manner that ensured equitable access for the community, as these communities had been dispersed or destroyed. Changing the way communities thought about land had changed the communities themselves. Embracing private property was therefore influenced by subdivision and potato dependence, as a result of the reorganisation of Ireland into commercial estates following the conquest.[36] Key to the development of the plantation economy was access to land: the displacement of communities facilitated the destruction of traditional tenure. The displacement of peasant communities to marginal areas in the West of Ireland gradually

[31] Ibid 162.
[32] Slater 172.
[33] Braa 204.
[34] Ibid 212.
[35] Ibid 213.
[36] Ibid.

severed their relationship with the land. Eventually, the communal mode of production disappeared, replaced by the capitalised agrarian sector. The conditions for the rejection of traditional tenure, however, were not inevitable outcomes of the working landscape, but the deliberate results of propertisation meant to detach communities from the land.

The commercialisation of land disrupted the existence of communities in tandem with the rhythms of local ecosystems. It was antithetical to the communal land ethos. Commercialisation encouraged subdivision, the introduction of conacre and cotter tenancies, priming the landscape for dissolution by making the subsistence base fragile, and the practice by colonial authorities of non-intervention during the Famine hastened the eradication of institutions and practices used to manage the land under rundale. Exceeding the limits of Irish land capacity accelerated agrarian production, but had devastating consequences for the soil, and the population. This was possible because ideas surrounding land as a subject of the market enabled the dismissal of land's natural limits and function as a medium for social connectivity for its traditional communities. This was a harbinger of the Famine, the dissolution of rundale, the rearrangement of peasant communities, and the consolidation of land under commercially oriented farmers.[37] The disappearance of the lineage mode of production signified the erasure of forms of labour defined by the interaction of nature, and social relations dependent upon these modes of labour. With the introduction of a new class structure, the agrarian society in Ireland was transformed. Cooperation and equity gave way to competition and increasingly individualised conceptions of land, which facilitated commodity production.[38] Dephysicalisation of land thus commodified people–place relations, defined solely by market exchange values.[39]

Underscoring the extent of alienation in the dephysicalised landscape is the complete dehumanisation of peoples who are disembodied in nature, thus becoming property themselves. Marx conceived of human beings as 'corporeal' beings, constituting a 'specific part of nature'.[40] The expropriation of nature on behalf of the capitalist class becomes the basis for the further expropriation and exploitation of humanity and nature, in a vicious cycle leading ultimately to a rupture in the metabolism of nature and society.[41] This is particularly evident in the slave colonies of the English-speaking Caribbean.

Marx observes that alienation commodifies not just land, but people. If land is no longer a landscape or place, then it follows that it is no longer peopled. Marx noted that in a world without people and without place, there

---

[37] Braa 213.
[38] Graham 152.
[39] Ibid.
[40] Marx, *Early Writings* at fn 184.
[41] Bellamy Foster and Clark, 'The Robbery of Nature' 17.

are only things.[42] This explains the comfort with which genocide was deployed as a policy in the Americas, as well as the creation of slave colonies in the Caribbean, where enslaved Africans as racialised chattel slaves were deprived of their humanity in the law. Planters drew slave supplies from Africa, which was home to diverse peoples of different linguistic, cultural and social backgrounds, which aided cultural assimilation and erasure in the New World.[43] Because enslaved Africans were so far removed from their places of origin, they were truly 'natally alienated', a phrase introduced by Orlando Patterson,[44] because they were alienated from their homeland, community and each other.

Enslaved Africans also had no connection to the Caribbean islands or the plantations in which they laboured. As strangers in a new land, with which they had no natural relationship, they were truly foreign. Marx's concept of human beings as part of nature demonstrates the mode by which enslaved Africans would be denied their humanity, as they belonged nowhere: neither Africa, nor the Caribbean. Natal alienation is therefore best understood as alienation from land.[45] This is the 'double injustice inherent in the slave-based plantation system: the denial of ownership of the land and the resulting denial of an identity, of a self, of an existence in the world'.[46] The commodification and fetishism of things through the prioritisation of exchange relations, resulting from the abstraction of land, things and people, reaches its nadir in the Caribbean, where the acceleration of capitalism required maximal exhaustion of nature and people.[47]

The ecosystems of the Caribbean were central to the region's transformation into slave colonies. A number of commodities that were in high demand in Europe, such as sugar, could not be grown locally. Sugar required certain climatic factors, and along with an assortment of plantation crops drove the evolution of the Atlantic plantation system, accelerated the growth of the slave trade, and anchored empire, particularly in Britain.[48] Caribbean geography would prove essential to sugar cultivation.[49] The Caribbean colonies, as

[42] Graham 135.

[43] George Beckford, *Persistent Poverty: Underdevelopment of Plantation Economies in the Third World* (Oxford University Press 1972) 38.

[44] Orlando Patterson, *Slavery and Social Death: A Comparative Study* (Harvard University Press 1982) 21–27; David Brion Davis, *Inhuman Bondage: The Rise and Fall of Slavery in the New World* (Oxford University Press 2008) 94.

[45] Olwig, 'Representation and Alienation' 20.

[46] Malcom Ferdinand, 'Ecology, Identity, and Colonialism in Martinique: The Discourse of an Ecological NGO (1980–2011)' in C Campbell and M Niblett (eds), *The Caribbean: Aesthetics, World-Ecology, Politics* (Liverpool University Press 2016) 174–188, 180.

[47] Jason W Moore, 'Transcending the Metabolic Rift: A Theory of Crises in the Capitalist World-Ecology' (2011) *The Journal of Peasant Studies* 38(1): 1–46, 19.

[48] William Beinart and Lotte Hughes, *Environment and Empire* (Oxford University Press 2009) 26 and 22.

[49] Mark W Hauser, 'A Political Ecology of Water and Enslavement' (2017) *Current Anthropology* 58(2): 227–256, 229, 233–234.

islands, were surrounded by the sea, and also had surface water, so plantations could rely on river channels for transporting goods.[50] Plantations demand vast areas of land, and the coastal tropical lowlands that were not densely populated proved an ideal fit. These lowlands were not permanently settled, but important to Amerindians who practiced shifting cultivation, a specific land use not immediately familiar to the arriving Europeans.[51] Improvement ideology had made its way to this region, as only those practicing settled agriculture could be considered legally entitled to claim sovereign rights over land, to improve it and optimise agricultural yields. The semi-nomadic Amerindian cultures,[52] who believed in a common or clan perception of landscape[53] were therefore subject to expropriation and colonisation.

Plantation agriculture in the Caribbean thus reassembled the landscapes of Amerindian peoples, and had catastrophic consequences for local ecosystems. The widespread conversion of these landscapes to plantations was fueled by perceptions of the Caribbean landscape as paradise, incapable of despoliation, and offering an eternal bounty of natural resources.[54] In some cases for small islands, the entire land mass could be deemed suitable for sugar cultivation. Capital-intensive plantation agriculture that was based on slave labour promoted detrimental environmental change in terms of deforestation, soil erosion, flooding, gullying, local aridification and drying up of streams and rivers.[55] The extreme land use and patterns of timber clearance made species recovery all but impossible, since their Native habitats were being transformed into sugar plantations.[56] In addition, transformations in industrial technology in the form of sugar mills and transport such as rail and shipping and associated port infrastructure were necessary to support the new industry.[57] At the end of the plantation agriculture period (1665–1833) in the English-speaking Caribbean, the lowland environment had been entirely depleted of nutrients and invaded by alien species.[58]

---

[50] Beinart and Hughes 23.

[51] Beckford 34.

[52] Ibid 286.

[53] Ibid 291.

[54] Jefferson Dillman, *Colonizing Paradise: Landscape and Empire in the British West Indies* (The University of Alabama Press 2015); Laura Hollsten, 'Controlling Nature and Transforming Landscapes in the Early Modern Caribbean' (2008) *Global Environment* 1(1): 80–113; Jill Casid, *Sowing Empire: Landscape and Colonization* (University of Minnesota Press 2004).

[55] Richard Grove, 'The Island and the History of Environmentalism' in Mikuláš Teich, Roy Porter and Bo Gustafsson (eds), *Nature and Society in Historical Context* (Cambridge University Press 1997) 150.

[56] Ibid.

[57] David Watts, *The West Indies: Patterns of Development Culture and Environmental Change since 1492* (Cambridge University Press 1990) 438.

[58] Ibid 443.

Natural resources were manipulated in such a manner as to entrench the planter/slave power dynamic,[59] which demanded permanent disruption of socio-ecological linkages in land. Over time, Amerindian peoples had been replaced by indentured European and then enslaved African labour. Enslaved populations existed to support the plantation system, which monopolised all natural resources. Enslaved Africans' association with nature therefore reaffirmed their lack of humanity, as their relationship with the land defined the extent of their oppression and exploitation. As legal property, they were chattels of the sugar estate, distinguishable from indentured labour, who could be freed and potentially acquire land. This racial distinction in the law, between enslaved Africans and Irish indentured servants, is first made in Barbados and exported thereafter throughout the British Empire.[60] A communal base was denied to enslaved Africans—they were not allowed to organise or form their own neighbourhoods. There were near insurmountable obstacles to the development of strong and well-defined societies in the Caribbean as the result of colonialism and the plantation system.[61] The decimation of Amerindians in the region (socially and politically) removed a common cultural base from which a population could rebuild and reassert itself, and enslaved Africans from diverse ethnicities and linguistic backgrounds was unable under the traumatic conditions of slavery to interact on their own terms and form sustainable communities.[62] Race and space are therefore implicated in the creation of property rights by emphasising detachment from nature in the law, a detachment that is accomplished through dispossession, genocide and dehumanisation.

The contrast between the slave-owner and the enslaved could not be starker when considered in spatial terms. The small planter elite, in the words of the historian Richard S. Dunn, 'held the best land, sold the most sugar, and monopolised the best offices. In only one generation these planters had turned their small island into an amazingly effective sugar-production machine

---

[59] Beinart and Hughes 37.

[60] In 1661 the Barbados House of Assembly passed two separate comprehensive labour codes: one act governed 'Christian Servants,' the other 'Negro slaves': 'An Act for the Better Ordering and Governing of Negroes,' September 27, 1661 (The National Archives, London, co 30/2, 16–26); 'An Act for the Good Governing of Servants, and Ordaining the Rights Between Masters and Servants' published in Richard Hall (ed), *1764. Acts, Passed in the Island of Barbados* (London: printed for Richard Hall) 35–42. See also Edward B Rugemer, 'The Development of Mastery and Race in the Comprehensive Slave Codes of the Greater Caribbean during the Seventeenth Century' (July 2013) *The William and Mary Quarterly* 70(3): 429–458.

[61] Mark W Hauser and Dan Hicks, 'Colonialism and Landscape: Power, Materiality and Scales of Analysis in Caribbean Historical Archaeology' in Dan Hicks, Laura McAtackney and Graham Fairclough (eds), *Envisioning Landscape: Situations and Standpoints in Archaeology and Heritage* (Routledge 2007) 253, 258; Beckford, *Persistent Poverty* 77.

[62] Beckford 77. It should be noted, however that enslaved Africans were able to challenge the plantation system in myriad ways, and the concept of agency within Caribbean plantation societies is thus a complex one.

and had built a social structure to rival the tradition-encrusted hierarchy of old England'.[63] Slave-owners, therefore, possessed spatial privileges in these islands as they held all property rights in land and labour, while slaves were physically emplaced but held no rights to exist outside the law.

Nevertheless, the population disparities concerned the white elite, who were surrounded by an enslaved majority. This encouraged the practice of absenteeism amongst the most powerful members of the plantocracy in the eighteenth and early nineteenth centuries.[64] A buffer class of professional 'book-keepers' (managers) and overseers was created to manage these estates. They in turn were motivated to maximise plantation profits in order to escape the region and retire home to Britain. This reinforced the perception that the region was 'uninhabitable', as there were no 'reassuring social and psychological boundaries of traditional societies'.[65]

Absentee slave-owners therefore were not even required to be in place or protect place while they owned land, sometimes multiple plantations across several islands. They held total control over the land, and the privileges that came with ownership, voting in the colonial legislatures, while living in England. It was to their benefit as property-owners that these slave colonies were not functioning places, and this dynamic was maintained to accrue and entrench their wealth. By contrast, enslaved populations were very much emplaced, shaping the land and developing complex enduring relations with the landscape, but their lived-in experiences found no formal expression in the law as they were owned rather than possessing ownership rights themselves. This dynamic has set the stage for modern capitalism's affinity with abstract property rights, often at the expense of lived-in landscapes and their inhabitants.

Public authorities entrenched the power of the plantocracy, even in their absence, because their sole function was to perpetuate the plantation system, which included regulation of life and work on the estates, and to ensure above all else that the enslaved population never challenged the status quo.[66] Legislation could not maximise profitability of plantation production and ensure the welfare of plantation labour at the same time.[67] It was thus antithetical to the survival of the slave colonies for legislation to recognise the humanity of

---

[63] Brion Davis 115. On the impact of the sugar industry see Sidney W Mintz, *Sweetness and Power: The Place of Sugar in Modern History* (Sifton 1985).

[64] Hicks 43–44.

[65] Brion Davis 115. The institution of slavery in the English-speaking Caribbean is discussed in Randy M Browne, *Surviving Slavery in the British Caribbean* (University of Pennsylvania Press 2017).

[66] Beckford 40.

[67] Ibid.

the slaves. 'The common law of England is the common law of the plantations', wrote the Admiralty's legal counsel, Richard West, in 1720.[68] That law deployed property rights as an ordering mechanism, unmaking landscapes and human interactions with nature in the process, which facilitated the degradation of both humanity and the environment.

Because no attention was paid to land as a base for human subsistence and identity, it was recognised only in terms of its market value. The dephysicalisation of land as vacuous space or paradise extinguished pre-existing Amerindian property rights in favour of private land ownership for the planter elite. Colonial property rights therefore facilitated the translation of these landscapes into property as we know it today and concretised particular cultural perceptions of land, nature and race so that they favoured maximum exploitation of people and the environment.

In critiquing capitalism and its impact through property rights on the natural limits of the land and the survival of mankind, Marx was in fact addressing the sustainability of property.[69] He articulated the costs of alienation that Bentham and Hohfeld never considered. He highlighted the underlying factors of spiritual estrangement, community displacement and environmental collapse that accompanied the dual process of alienation, severing nature from culture. That alienation is no longer considered a rupture in the fabric of the landscape, but a process of agency, helmed by individual property owners who can alienate tradeable rights in land, demonstrates the successful dephysicalisation of the landscape. Marx never referred to the term landscape, but in recognising local ecological limits, he considered the spatial consequences of alienation on communities that were dispossessed or displaced from the nature to which they belonged. Such a treatment is absent in Hohfeldian property theory where property is an abstract right.

Exceeding the limits of Irish land's natural capacity had devastating consequences leading to the Famine. The policy of non-intervention, reflected in laws and practices at the time, conceived of soil exhaustion as natural shocks in the economy, which would right itself in due course. No attention was paid to land as the basis for cultural life, so the Famine indirectly destroyed traditional communities by destroying communal modes of production and inheritance. In the Caribbean, ecosystem collapse was an inevitable result of the dephysicalisation of the landscape. The comprehensive propertisation of Caribbean landscapes demanded the dissolution of Amerindian property and the dehumanisation of enslaved African peoples to ensure the rift between man and nature was maintained.

---

[68] Richard West, 'On English Common and Statute Law in Settled Colonies' (June 1720) in Madden and Fieldhouse (eds), *Select Documents on the Constitutional History of the British Empire and Commonwealth* (4 vols., Westport, Conn 1985) 2, 192, as cited in Eliga Gould, 'Zones of Law, Zones of Violence: The Legal Geography of the British Atlantic, circa 1772' (July 2003) *The William and Mary Quarterly* 60(3): 471–510, 497.

[69] Graham 98.

Marx's regard for the 'conscious and sustainable regulation of the metabolic interaction between humanity and nature'[70] reflects an understanding of the inherent logic of the landscape. Marx rejected linear approaches to agriculture's development, enabling him to recognise modern agriculture's irrational and destructive use of land.[71] In situating alienation within its natural and social context, Marx demonstrated the costs of propertisation of the landscape. He resisted ahistoric and aspatial approaches to land, recognised the human, social and ecological costs of alienation not addressed today, and the fissuring of the landscape (through the division of its socio-cultural and ecological elements) as the critical event facilitating land's ultimate abstraction or propertisation—its final conceptualisation as a bundle of transferable rights or property.[72]

References

G Beckford, *Persistent Poverty: Underdevelopment of Plantation Economies in the Third World* (Oxford University Press 1972).

W Beinart and L Hughes, *Environment and Empire* (Oxford University Press 2009).

J Bellamy Foster, 'The Rediscovery of Marx's Ecology' in Marcello Musto (ed), *The Marx Revival: Key Concepts and New Interpretations* (Cambridge 2020).

J Bellamy Foster and Brett Clark, 'The Robbery of Nature: Capitalism and the Metabolic Rift' (July–August 2018) *Monthly Review* 7(3): 1–20.

J Bellamy Foster and B Clark, 'The Rift of Eire' (April 2020) *Monthly Review* 71(11): 1–11.

DM Braa, 'The Great Potato Famine and the Transformation of Irish Peasant Society' (1997) *Science & Society* 61(2): 193–215.

D Brion Davis, *Inhuman Bondage: The Rise and Fall of Slavery in the New World* (Oxford University Press 2008).

RM Browne, *Surviving Slavery in the British Caribbean* (University of Pennsylvania Press 2017).

J Casid, *Sowing Empire: Landscape and Colonization* (University of Minnesota Press 2004).

J Dillman, *Colonizing Paradise: Landscape and Empire in the British West Indies* (University of Alabama Press 2015).

A Dowling, 'Of Ships and Sealing Wax: The Introduction of Land Registration in Ireland' (1993) *Northern Ireland Legal Quarterly* 44: 360–380.

---

[70] Saito 39.

[71] Saito 28.

[72] The land registration system which emerged around the time of Marx's writing was based on models designed for government stock and shipping, and was meant to make land as easily transferable as any other property. Sir Robert Torrens later said of the system he created that he 'copied the whole system from the transfer of shipping' (Report of Her Majesty's Commissioners oil Agriculture (1881) BPP xiv I, App q 65.484. See Alan Dowling, 'Of Ships and Sealing Wax: The Introduction of Land Registration in Ireland' (1993) *N Ir Legal Q* 44: 360–380, 360 and 364.

M Ferdinand, 'Ecology, Identity, and Colonialism in Martinique: The Discourse of an Ecological NGO (1980–2011)' in C Campbell and M Niblett (eds), *The Caribbean: Aesthetics, World-Ecology, Politics* (Liverpool University Press 2016) 174–188.

E Gould, 'Zones of Law, Zones of Violence: The Legal Geography of the British Atlantic, circa 1772' (July 2003) *The William and Mary Quarterly* 60(3): 471–510.

N Graham, *Lawscape: Property, Environment, Law* (Routledge-Cavendish 2010).

R Grove, 'The Island and the History of Environmentalism' in M Teich, R Porter and B Gustafsson (eds), *Nature and Society in Historical Context* (Cambridge University Press 1997).

R Hall (ed), *1764. Acts, Passed in the Island of Barbados* (London: printed for Richard Hall).

MW Hauser, 'A Political Ecology of Water and Enslavement' (2017) *Current Anthropology* 58(2): 227–256.

MW Hauser and D Hicks, 'Colonialism and Landscape: Power, Materiality and Scales of Analysis in Caribbean Historical Archaeology' in D Hicks, L McAtackney and G Fairclough (eds), *Envisioning Landscape: Situations and Standpoints in Archaeology and Heritage* (Routledge 2007).

D Hicks, L McAtackney and G Fairclough (eds), *Envisioning Landscape: Situations and Standpoints in Archaeology and Heritage* (Routledge 2007).

L Hollsten, 'Controlling Nature and Transforming Landscapes in the Early Modern Caribbean' (2008) *Global Environment* 1(1): 80–113.

K Marx, *Grundrisse* (Penguin 1973).

_____, *Capital* (vol. 1, Penguin 1976).

_____, 'Outline of a Report on the Irish Question to the Communist Educational Association of German Workers in London, December 16, 1867' in K Marx and F Engels (eds), *Ireland and the Irish Question* (Moscow 1978).

_____, *Early Writings* (Penguin 1992).

SW Mintz, *Sweetness and Power: The Place of Sugar in Modern History* (Sifton 1985).

JW Moore, 'Transcending the Metabolic Rift: A Theory of Crises in the Capitalist World-Ecology' (2011) *The Journal of Peasant Studies* 38(1): 1–46.

K Olwig, 'Representation and Alienation in the Political Landscape' (2005) *Cultural Geographies* 12(1): 19–40.

O Patterson, *Slavery and Social Death: A Comparative Study* (Harvard University Press 1982) 21–27.

EB Rugemer, 'The Development of Mastery and Race in the Comprehensive Slave Codes of the Greater Caribbean during the Seventeenth Century' (July 2013) *The William and Mary Quarterly* 70(3): 429–458.

K Saito, 'Marx's Ecological Notebooks' (February 2016) *Monthly Review* 67(9): 25–42.

E Slater and T McDonough, 'Marx on Nineteenth-Century Colonial Ireland: Analysing Colonialism as a Dynamic Social Process' (November 2008) *Irish Historical Studies* 36(142): 153–172.

E Slater and E Flaherty, 'Marx on Primitive Communism: The Irish Rundale Agrarian Commune, Its Internal Dynamics and the Metabolic Rift' (2009) *Irish Journal of Anthropology* 12(2): 5–34.

RC Tucker (ed), *The Marx - Engels Reader* (2nd edn., W.W. Norton & Company 1978).

S Vogel, 'Marx and Alienation from Nature' (1988) *Social Theory and Practice* 14(3): 367–387.

D Watts, *The West Indies: Patterns of Development, Culture and Environmental Change since 1492* (Cambridge University Press 1990).
R West, 'On English Common and Statute Law in Settled Colonies' (June 1720) in Madden and Fieldhouse(eds), *Select Documents on the Constitutional History of the British Empire and Commonwealth* (4 vols., Westport, Conn 1985).

Open Access This chapter is licensed under the terms of the Creative Commons Attribution 4.0 International License (http://creativecommons.org/licenses/by/4.0/), which permits use, sharing, adaptation, distribution and reproduction in any medium or format, as long as you give appropriate credit to the original author(s) and the source, provide a link to the Creative Commons license and indicate if changes were made.

The images or other third party material in this chapter are included in the chapter's Creative Commons license, unless indicated otherwise in a credit line to the material. If material is not included in the chapter's Creative Commons license and your intended use is not permitted by statutory regulation or exceeds the permitted use, you will need to obtain permission directly from the copyright holder.

CHAPTER 6

Extinguishing Landscape, Creating Property: Property and Spatial Injustice

Abstract This chapter reflects on the ways in which loss of place or landscape destruction can be considered intrinsic to property's formulation in the law. In summarising the relationship between the common law and land by examining property's impact on various geographic locations, it becomes clear that private property has benefitted from undemocratic and environmentally harmful activities that have concerning implications for sustainable land use. Failure to consider enduring people–place relations developed in response to local limits means that property operates without regard for the physical environment, including its cultural dimensions, and this has implications for human rights and ecological resilience. The chapter closes by identifying this transition from landscape to property as spatial injustice that is upheld by the law.

Keywords Abstract logic · Landscape destruction · Spatial injustice · Cultural dimension of land

Property has been abstracted to the point where it is illusory.[1] Indeed, Margaret Davies denounces property by stating:

> It is evidence of the perniciousness and emptiness of this concept of property that it is extendable equally to a person (through the now-defunct concept of

---

[1] Kevin Gray, 'Property in Thin Air' (1991) *Cambridge Law Journal* 50: 252–307, 306: 'When subjected to close analysis the concept of "property" vanishes into thin air just as surely and elusively as the desired phantom with which we began'.

slavery) and to a plastic bucket, and that it can imagine land as two-dimensional space without ecological characteristics or heritage.[2]

This abstract logic of property is symptomatic of the law's perceived impartiality, which relies on the denial of geography to be universally applicable. Yet, acknowledgement of geographic disparities is central to spatial justice. It follows that property's ascendancy coincides with the destruction of landscapes, which were defined by locally specific uses and interests in land.

The accretion of private property rights in the common law thus required the elimination of the social and cultural dimensions of land. Locke, Blackstone and Marx were not familiar with landscape as a legal geographical concept, but their contributions to property theory are relevant to the integrity of land. Locke focused on the individual using his labour to transform the commons into private property. This influenced the perception of common resources, the core of the working landscape, as primitive, undeveloped and homogenous. Garret Hardin's influential article on the 'Tragedy of the Commons',[3] relied on this misconception of the commons as an open resource situation inherently incapable of management, while positioning private property as its superior alternative, though Hardin later recanted and revised this thesis.[4]

Enclosure of common land was achieved through Parliament (the Enclosure Acts) and the courts. This had far-reaching biogeographic and social consequences, facilitating the decline of diverse communally managed areas in England. The American colonies in particular served as the loci for Locke's theories of land acquisition and property, where commons were 'wasted' and required individual improvement to generate maximum profit. At home and abroad, enclosing land served to flatten ecosystems, interests and communities into the imperial landscape from which property rights could be created. European settlers ejected Native Americans from their own land in violent and oppressive ways, also masked as legal transfers on the land market.

Like Locke, Blackstone was well versed in the fluidity of interests in land and discussed them in his chapter on tenures.[5] However, Blackstone relied on medieval legal sources on feudalism to legitimise the common law,

---

[2] Davies 1110.

[3] *Science* (1968) 162(3859): 1243–1248.

[4] Garrett Hardin, 'The Tragedy of the 'Unmanaged' Commons' in RV Andelson (ed), *Commons Without Tragedy* (Shepheard Walwyn 1991). However, Oosthuizen points out that Hardin conflated public property rights with common rights, and this thesis was debunked by S Ciriacy-Wantrup and Richard C Bishop '"Common Property" as a Concept in Natural Resources Policy' (1975) *Natural Resources Journal* 15: 713–727. See also Oosthuizen on the archaeological evidence for effectively functioning common property rights in early medieval England in *The Emergence of the English* (Arc Humanities Press 2019).

[5] 1 Bl Comm 59; Carol M Rose, 'Canons of Property Talk, or, Blackstone's Anxiety' (1998) *The Yale Law Journal* 108: 601–632, 603.

contrasting feudal Norman values with ostensibly liberal, enlightened English ones. He paid scant attention to local lived-in land practices and customs in England, denoting them encumbrances against the landlord, which impaired his ability to exercise full possession and enjoyment of the land. These uses were no longer proto-regulatory mechanisms developed by commoners to ensure their independent way of life, but constraints or burdens upon the private landowner. Blackstone thus contextualised the development of property as deliverance from the 'slavery' of feudalism and viewed the assertion of private property rights through the right to exclude as an attempt to restore the original liberties of the Saxon constitution.[6]

Marx, unlike Blackstone, emphasised the social relations that belied the tenurial system in feudal England, and examined the costs of the loss of these mutual social relations when people were dispossessed of land, now celebrated as a key characteristic of property: alienability. Land's capacity for alienation accompanies the abstraction of land or the complete extinguishment of the landscape. The starting point is the dephysicalisation or rift between people and nature. Marx questioned the ecological costs of capitalism through its deployment of property rights in the accumulation of wealth. In his critique of capitalism and the idea of the metabolic rift, Marx addressed the concept and impact of the human loss of place-defined relationships in land. Colonies such as Ireland and those in the Caribbean found themselves at the frontier of capitalism, where land was exploited beyond its physical limits. The metabolic rift thus occurs when land has been so dephysicalised that there are no limits to exceed—and this enabled the ecological collapse that preceded Ireland's Famine and the destruction of Caribbean island ecosystems and societies via plantation agriculture.

These examples of landscape destruction were accomplished through the delineation and imposition of property rights. The emphasis on law's abstract logic enabled the dismissal of geographical disparities wherever property was deployed. This is demonstrated by the inability of land law in various jurisdictions to respond to locally specific conditions, resulting in spatial injustice. But, it is difficult to challenge property when it acts as a filter constraining the way land itself is understood. Private property rights are aligned with liberal democracy, impoverishing property discourse by framing private property as the ideal institution keeping repressive monarchy at bay at one end of the spectrum, while avoiding collectivist agriculture models imposed by the State at the other.[7]

The inability to recognise distinctive communal land regimes explains the continuing failure of the law to regulate the commons adequately, since prescribed management mechanisms treat all commons as homogenous and

---

[6] Burns 79; 2 Bl Comm 51–52.
[7] Ellickson 1318.

interchangeable.[8] The influence of the American concept of wilderness on international cultural heritage law and environmental law can be seen in the protection of national parks around the world that were often originally lived-in landscapes from which Native peoples had been expelled, as was the case with Yosemite and Yellowstone National Parks.[9] Privatisation of public space has spatial implications, especially in small island states where developers view land as a commercial asset, and planning permission is often granted without considering non-ownership interests of local communities that affect their livelihoods and continued existence.

Landscape now exists only in the scenic sense (such as a landscaped garden) because its representative qualities for the community have been reduced to the pictorial. Other ways of construing land have not been extended beyond the Indigenous context, which means that the law treats collective understandings of land as an exception. Attempts at defining collective or communal land practices are often fixed in time, imposed from the top down (the écomusée model of a heritage landscape) or performative (a commune) or are absorbed into ethno-nationalist extremist views.[10] These all fail to capture the dynamic sense of the flexible working landscape as a nexus of land, law and people.

References

W Blackstone, *Commentaries on the Laws of England* (Oxford 1765–1769).
RP Burns, 'Blackstone's Theory of the Absolute Rights of Property' (1985) *University of Cincinnati Law Review* 54: 67–87.
S Ciriacy-Wantrup and Richard C Bishop '"Common Property" as a Concept in Natural Resources Policy' (1975) *Natural Resources Journal* 15: 713–727.
A Clarke, 'How Property Works: The Complex World View' (2013) *Nottingham Law Journal* 22: 141–155.
M Davies, 'Can Property Be Justified in an Entangled World?' (2020) *Globalizations* 17(7): 1104–1117.
RC Ellickson, 'Property in Land' (1993) *The Yale Law Journal* 102(6): 1315–1400.
K Gray, 'Property in Thin Air' (1991) *Cambridge Law Journal* 50: 252–307.
G Hardin, 'Tragedy of the Commons' (1968) *Science* 162(3859): 1243–1248.
———, 'The Tragedy of the "Unmanaged" Commons' in RV Andelson (ed), *Commons Without Tragedy* (Shepheard Walwyn 1991).
K Olwig, *Landscape, Nature and the Body Politic: From Britain's Renaissance to America's New World* (University of Wisconsin Press 2002).
S Oosthuizen, *The Emergence of the English* (Arc Humanities Press 2019).

---

[8] Alison Clarke, on the failure of the English Commons Registration Act 1965, partially remedied by the Commons Act 2006, in 'How Property Works: The Complex World view' (2013) *Nottingham L.J.* 22: 141–155, 149.

[9] David Treuer, 'Return the National Parks to the Tribes' (*The Atlantic* May 2021) accessed 29 May 2021, https://www.theatlantic.com/magazine/archive/2021/05/return-the-national-parks-to-the-tribes/618395/; Olwig, *Landscape Nature and the Body Politic* 224.

[10] Olwig *Landscape, Nature and the Body Politic* 226.

CM Rose, 'Canons of Property Talk, or, Blackstone's Anxiety' (1998) *The Yale Law Journal* 108: 601–632.

D Treuer, 'Return the National Parks to the Tribes' (*The Atlantic* May 2021) accessed 29 May 2021, https://wwwtheatlantic.commagazine/archive/2021/05/return-the-national-parks-to-the-tribes/618395/.

Open Access This chapter is licensed under the terms of the Creative Commons Attribution 4.0 International License (http://creativecommons.org/licenses/by/4.0/), which permits use, sharing, adaptation, distribution and reproduction in any medium or format, as long as you give appropriate credit to the original author(s) and the source, provide a link to the Creative Commons license and indicate if changes were made.

The images or other third party material in this chapter are included in the chapter's Creative Commons license, unless indicated otherwise in a credit line to the material. If material is not included in the chapter's Creative Commons license and your intended use is not permitted by statutory regulation or exceeds the permitted use, you will need to obtain permission directly from the copyright holder.

CHAPTER 7

Progressive Property: A Spatially Just Approach to Property?

Abstract This chapter examines the progressive property school's attempts to address property's shortcomings, as it is one of the more recent critiques of the ownership model to have gained traction. The main characteristics of progressive property are described, and the contributions of prominent scholars are summarised in relation to virtue ethics, public trust and the common heritage of mankind. While noting that this school emerged in the specific cultural context of the US, and that its parameters are continuing to evolve, the chapter nevertheless outlines some conceptual limitations in progressive property thinking that have implications for developing a spatially just approach to property. The chapter concludes by reinforcing the importance of a legal geographical perspective when examining the law's relationship with land.

Keywords Progressive property · Ownership · Virtue ethics · Public trust doctrine · Common heritage of mankind

The progressive property school of thought has attempted to challenge the ownership model and its grip on property. In a statement, four leading scholars outlined its main tenets.[1] These include the recognition that because property confers power and reallocates resources, it has the ability to alter social relationships and impact communities;[2] property as a social institution should thus

---

[1] Gregory S Alexander, Eduardo M Peñalver, Joseph W Singer and Laura S Underkuffler, 'A Statement of Progressive Property' (2009) *Cornell Law Review* 94: 743–745.

[2] Laura S Underkuffler, 'The Holy Grail of Progressive Property' (2020) *Cornell Journal of Law and Public Policy* 29: 717–735, 719.

© The Author(s) 2023
A. Byer, *Placing Property*, Palgrave Socio-Legal Studies,
https://doi.org/10.1007/978-3-031-31994-5_7

meet underlying moral values[3] and support a free and democratic society.[4] Such a model would apply values consistent with human flourishing, and be responsive to the effects of claiming property rights on others, including the environment and the non-human world.[5] Here, I briefly consider whether the conceptual possibilities afforded by progressive property are sufficiently transformative to incorporate spatial justice.

As Timothy Mulvaney writes, progressive property scholars 'offer an alternative to what they see as the currently dominant conception of property that is heavily centered on coordinating economic transactions and for which standardised exclusion rights constitute ownership's essential core'.[6] Thus, property law making 'must be more nuanced, more expressly political, and less preoccupied with the owner's right to exclude'.[7] An understanding that ownership does not countenance alternative understandings of property (thus failing to accept property's plural values), challenging the Demsetzian concept of economic maximisation as it relates to land[8] and promoting social justice appear to characterise this scholarship.

This has led to several strands of research, including an investigation of property's roots in Anglo-American law which predate the market and were previously aligned to a notion of social good,[9] revealing that non-owners can build up long-standing attachments to land over time[10] and promoting a new normative framework for land use based on virtue ethics.[11] However, critics have questioned the use of virtue ethics where human beings demonstrate that they can be situational ethical,[12] and whether using law to promote virtue is consistent with society's value pluralism.[13] Property theorists have also posited that property can play a constituent role in identity formation,[14] but this is

---

[3] Patrick JL Cockburn, 'A Common Sense of Property?' (2016) *Distinktion: Journal of Social Theory* 17(1): 78–79, 85.

[4] 'A Statement of Progressive Property' 744.

[5] Ibid.

[6] Timothy Mulvaney, 'Progressive Property Moving Forward' (2014) *California Law Review* 5: 349–373, 351.

[7] Ezra Rosser, 'The Ambition and Transformative Potential of Progressive Property' (February 2013) *California Law Review* 101(1): 107–171, 109–110.

[8] Harold Demsetz, 'Toward a Theory of Property Rights' (1967) *American Economic Review* 57: 347–359.

[9] Gregory Alexander, 'Property as Propriety' (1998) *Nebraska Law Review* 77: 667–699.

[10] Joseph William Singer, 'The Reliance Interest in Property' (1988) *Stanford Law Review* 40: 611–751, 622.

[11] Eduardo M. Peñalver, 'Land Virtues' (2009) *Cornell Law Review* 94: 821–889.

[12] Katrina Wyman, 'Should Property Scholars Embrace Virtue Ethics—A Skeptical Comment' (2009) *Cornell Law Review* 94: 991–1008, 1000, 1002.

[13] Wyman 1003.

[14] Margaret Radin, 'Property and Personhood' (1982) *Stanford Law Review* 34(5): 957–1015.

conceived of in individualistic terms, rather than spatial ones.[15] There have been attempts to apply property as identity, but strictly as it applies to Indigenous peoples and the experience of dispossession of land within the settler colonial context.[16]

Absent in the discussions is the role of the land itself, and the attendant relationships that emanate from human interaction with the environment. These are not monolithic. Morality is not recognised as spatially embedded in the landscape as it evolved from the mores and use rights of local custom. Common customary law wielded power through moral pressure and community control, which protected shared resources from deterioration and loss.[17] A universal morality may possess rhetorical force, but without a focus on lived-in people–place relations, the relevance of locally encoded behaviour to ecosystem protection will be overlooked.[18]

In addition, both the welfare function of property and the goal of human flourishing are informed by locally specific factors of geography as they manifest in the physical environment. Geographic disparities can define and exacerbate inequalities in public health, housing and food security. In fact, inequalities stem from the distribution of land, which differs from place to place. Terms such as 'moral', 'welfare', 'flourishing', 'resource' and 'environment', are therefore subject to heterotopian formulation, not accounted for in progressive property theory.

Society is composed of communities generating their own norms that can challenge and vary how property operates, rather than a generic public. Resources are also not generic, and the term itself implies extractability and exploitability, which does not encompass cultural understandings of land. Thinking of resources in terms of water, land, oil, minerals entrenches the alienability of land, not as a web of interacting rights, interests and uses but as separable strands easily teased out and exchangeable on the market. Arbitrary application of terms such as 'common heritage of mankind' elides the locally developed relationships that can be critical to the continued functioning of places. While the use of the public trust doctrine is claimed as a strength in unifying people with the environment under progressive property,[19] it in fact demonstrates the limits of what property can do where lived-in places are

---

[15] Edward Soja, *Seeking Spatial Justice* (University of Minnesota Press 2010).

[16] See Kristin Carpenter's work, which has extended Radin's model to identity in terms of collective peoplehood: K Carpenter, 'Real Property and Peoplehood' (2008) *Stanford Environmental Law Journal* 27: 313–396.

[17] See Olwig, 'Virtual Enclosure, Ecosystem Services, Landscape's Character and the 'Rewilding' of the Commons: the 'Lake District' Case' *Landscape Research* 41(2): 253–264, 256.

[18] See Nicholas Blomley, 'Performing Property: Making the World' (2013) *The Canadian Journal of Law & Jurisprudence* 26: 23–48.

[19] Laura Spitz and Eduardo M Peñalver, 'Nature's Personhood and Property's Virtues' (2021) *Harvard Environmental Law Review* 45: 67–98, 94.

concerned, because it is defined in terms of ownership, serving the general public interest and for fixed purposes.[20]

Landscape or place is therefore the omission in progressive property's attempts to reconcile the public trust doctrine with the environment, particularly as this doctrine derives from Roman law and notions of state-owned property for the benefit of all its citizens, common to all or owned by all (communes omnibus and communes omnium respectively).[21] It was not concerned with local interests in land. Modifying or balancing ownership prerogatives continues to rely on the assumption that private ownership can accommodate and respond to generic resources that exist to be exploited rationally via the market, rather than interconnected ecosystems that rely on place-specific communal interaction for continued functioning. Protecting resources, even in ostensibly sustainable ways, does not negate the extractable logic of property rights that facilitated dispossession and despoliation of land in the first place, particularly where those resources were perceived to be scarce.

While progressive scholars have indeed drawn attention to property's limits in the social sphere, it is difficult to transcend private property, which is still aligned with individual freedom while the collective remains a homogenous interest. Non-ownership interests in land remain subordinate to property or are completely absent. Where redistribution is promoted, it is not clear that this involves communal understandings of land, which might vary from community to community. The intention is to 'dissolve the baseline that private property exists primarily to advantage owners and create market gains (or, even, for that matter, to promote freedom) in favor of a system of property that regularly realigns so that it remains justified in terms of the widespread benefits it offers to the collective'.[22] This interpretation might lend itself to the idea that individual property necessitates encumbrances in the name of welfare, a modern variation on Blackstone. In modifying individual ownership to achieve social justice goals for the collective, assumptions are made about the collective that ignore geography, and could ultimately undermine the integrity of place. Progressive property is thus hampered by its lack of place literacy.

However, it must be acknowledged that the main exponents of progressive property, thus far have been mostly American and concerned with the history, ethos and problems of land use in the United States. In the United Kingdom and Ireland, scholars drawing on legal realism and legal geography have begun to engage with the notion of property as abstract and reflect on

[20] Spitz and Peñalver 95.

[21] See Bruce W Frier, 'The Roman Origins of the Public Trust Doctrine' (October 14, 2019). The University of Michigan Public Law Research Paper No. 655, *Journal of Roman Archaeology* 32. Carol Rose notes that Joseph Sax extended the public trust concept, originally concerned with bodies of water, to land and natural resource management in general. See Rose, 'Joseph Sax and the Idea of the Public Trust' (1998) *Ecology Law Quarterly* 25: 351–362.

[22] Mulvaney 368.

the consequences for informal, lived-in relationships with land.[23] Land law in particular has been noted to be the body of law most committed to legal doctrinalism, and as a result, pays little attention to the ways in which people can be marginalised and rendered invisible through the reinforcement of legal norms.[24] This challenges the presumed neutrality of property and exposes the distorting effects of the ownership model on land.

In spite of these promising advances, progressive property scholarship has not replaced the existing normative framework. Thus far, there is simply no vocabulary for articulating the functions of landscape in the common law—it is an outlier in property law. In fact, landscape's functions have been redistributed to other areas of law, such as cultural heritage law, planning law and environmental law, which act as proxies that reinforce the property concept by managing conflicts over custom, land use and environmental impacts in ways that insulate private property rights from challenges.

Propertising the landscape has thus contributed to spatial injustice—property as a narrative, as an institution and as a concept inhibits diverse understandings of land that align with physical reality, represent pluralistic values and respect non-ownership interests in land.

References

G Alexander, 'Property as Propriety' (1998) *Nebraska Law Review* 77: 667–699.
GS Alexander, EM Peñalver, JW Singer and LS Underkuffler 'A Statement of Progressive Property' (2009) *Cornell Law Review* 94: 743–745.
S Blandy, S Bright and S Nield, 'The Dynamics of Enduring Property Relationships in Land' (2018) *Modern Law Review* 81(1): 85–113.
N Blomley, 'Performing Property: Making the World' (2013) *Canadian Journal of Law & Jurisprudence* 26: 23–48.
K Carpenter, 'Real Property and Peoplehood' (2008) *Stanford Environmental Law Journal* 27: 313–396.
PJL Cockburn, 'A Common Sense of Property?' (2016) *Distinktion: Journal of Social Theory* 17(1): 78–93.
H Demsetz, 'Toward a Theory of Property Rights' (1967) *American Economic Review* 57: 347–359.
L Fox O'Mahony, 'Property Outsiders and the Hidden Politics of Doctrinalism' (2014) *Current Legal Problems* 67(1): 409–445.
BW Frier, 'The Roman Origins of the Public Trust Doctrine' (October 14, 2019). University of Michigan Public Law Research Paper No. 655, *Journal of Roman Archaeology* 32.
T Mulvaney, 'Progressive Property Moving Forward' (2014) *California Law Review* 5: 349–373.

---

[23] Sarah Blandy, Susan Bright and Sarah Nield, 'The Dynamics of Enduring Property Relationships in Land' (2018) *Modern Law Review* 81(1): 85–113. See also Rachael Walsh, *Property Rights and Social Justice: Progressive Property in Action* (Cambridge 2021).

[24] Lorna Fox O'Mahony, 'Property Outsiders and the Hidden Politics of Doctrinalism' (2014) *Current Legal Problems* 67: 409–445, 419, 414.

K Olwig, 'Virtual Enclosure, Ecosystem Services, Landscape's Character and the "Rewilding" of the Commons: The "Lake District" Case' (2016) *Landscape Research* 41(2): 253–264.

EM Peñalver, 'Land Virtues' (2009) *Cornell Law Review* 94: 821–889.

M Radin, 'Property and Personhood' (1982) *Stanford Law Review* 34(5): 957–1015.

C Rose, 'Joseph Sax and the Idea of the Public Trust' (1998) *Ecology Law Quarterly* 25: 351–362.

E Rosser, 'The Ambition and Transformative Potential of Progressive Property' (2013) *California Law Review* 101(1): 107–171.

JW Singer, 'The Reliance Interest in Property' (1988) *Stanford Law Review* 40: 611–751.

E Soja, *Seeking Spatial Justice* (University of Minnesota Press 2010).

L Spitz and EM Peñalver, 'Nature's Personhood and Property's Virtues' (2021) *Harvard Environmental Law Review* 45: 67–98.

LS Underkuffler, 'The Holy Grail of Progressive Property' (2020) *Cornell Journal of Law and Public Policy* 29: 717–735.

Rachael Walsh, *Property Rights and Social Justice: Progressive Property in Action* (Cambridge 2021).

K Wyman, 'Should Property Scholars Embrace Virtue Ethics—A Skeptical Comment' (2009) *Cornell Law Review* 94: 991–1008.

Open Access This chapter is licensed under the terms of the Creative Commons Attribution 4.0 International License (http://creativecommons.org/licenses/by/4.0/), which permits use, sharing, adaptation, distribution and reproduction in any medium or format, as long as you give appropriate credit to the original author(s) and the source, provide a link to the Creative Commons license and indicate if changes were made.

The images or other third party material in this chapter are included in the chapter's Creative Commons license, unless indicated otherwise in a credit line to the material. If material is not included in the chapter's Creative Commons license and your intended use is not permitted by statutory regulation or exceeds the permitted use, you will need to obtain permission directly from the copyright holder.

CHAPTER 8

Conclusion: Property's Placelessness

Abstract The closing chapter recaps the book's objectives, which were to determine property's origins, now identified in pre-feudal landscape, recover the spatial parameters of the theories of Locke, Blackstone and Marx, which are foundational to classical property theory, and highlight the process of converting landscapes to property as an exercise in spatial injustice that is facilitated by the law. This process was not linear or progressive, in response to land's environmental limits, but executed through enclosure, displacement and colonisation. As a result, the chapter contends that a legal geographical perspective reveals that property is based on detachment from place, and this placelessness has implications for sustainable land use today.

Keywords Landscape · Placelessness · Legal geography · Spatial injustice · Property

This book has expanded the critique of property, situating property's origins not in Lockean political economy, but in prefeudal landscape, a matrix of custom, commons and land use. By incorporating landscape and its relation to property in the analysis of the conceptualisation of land in the common law, I considered the spatial implications of the classic hallmarks of property—individual, exclusive and abstract tradeable rights—through an examination of the contributions of foundational thinkers on property—Locke, Blackstone and Marx. In particular, I assessed Marx's ecological critique of property rights and land in legal geographical terms.

Property diverged from its collective place-based origins, not as a result of a linear evolutionary process, or a response to natural changes in the physical world, but rather as a deliberate policy choice, executed through enclosure, colonisation and displacement. These practices were facilitated by the common law system as it gradually retreated from grounded perspectives on land in favour of abstract rights that were spatially unjust in effect. When landscape was homogenised, its distinctiveness was ascribed to individuals as the force behind acceptable land use rather than the community–environment dynamic; when its social functions were externalised, it became capable of exclusive possession, as other uses of the land become burdens, privileges or embellishments, permissible only at the discretion of the landowner when previously intrinsic to the land's character; and when it was severed from nature or dephysicalised, landscape transcended its natural limits, becoming alienable and tradeable as a commodity to one and all.

The scale of land dispossession and the acceleration of environmental degradation have concentrated themselves within the last two hundred years of human existence, coinciding with property's ascendance. But the spatially unjust effects of the enclosure of the commons, plantation monoculture, Native genocide and slavery in the longue duree are easily obscured by the law's neutral conceptualisation of property rights for sale on the global market. While property has been limited and adapted over the centuries, its central features remain, and continue to resist emplacement, valuing placelessness above all else.

The law regulates the use and access of land, and so plays a vital role in sustainable land use. However, the law defines land in terms of ownership, which is detached from the physical reality of land, land-based relations and functions that relate to people, species and ecosystems. This detachment has served to distort the understanding of land, which is ironic, since property originally encompassed socio-cultural and ecological functions of land when it was integrated with landscape. Property as currently configured therefore constrains our ability to see land beyond ownership, eschewing such insights in favour of technical solutions that are State-driven and entrench commercial and elite interests in land. Yet, we cannot transcend the limits of land. Property rights have stimulated industry, advances in technology, as well as the accumulation of wealth and the distribution of benefits to society. However, property rights have arisen in undemocratic and ecologically destructive circumstances that continue to threaten sustainable land use today, welcoming all benefits of land use while transferring the costs of private ownership as externalities to the wider public. This is not tenable, and we have to contend with the implications of conceiving property in isolation from the landscape.

Landscape is an antidote to this thinking because it offers a counternarrative to the homogenising, universalising and interchangeable nature of property rights. Acknowledging dynamic, evolving, non-ownership interests in land offers a perspective that embraces land in all its dimensions, aligning with the reality of diversity in people, ecosystems and biota.

When land is treated as abstract space by the law, there are profound implications for communities, ecosystems and planetary boundaries. Ownership is too narrow a filter for defining and managing land when land security is of global concern. Re-engagement with the landscape could offer a comprehensive and materially relevant understanding of the land, and challenge property's placelessness.

The deficiency of this conceptualisation of land as property however is only fully evident through a legal geographical lens. Embedding law within its geographic reality emphasises the absence of landscapes, through the alienation of peoples and environments that contribute to and define the land in all its complexity. A critique of property law thus necessitates this examination of the divergence between landscape and property.

Open Access This chapter is licensed under the terms of the Creative Commons Attribution 4.0 International License (http://creativecommons.org/licenses/by/4.0/), which permits use, sharing, adaptation, distribution and reproduction in any medium or format, as long as you give appropriate credit to the original author(s) and the source, provide a link to the Creative Commons license and indicate if changes were made.

The images or other third party material in this chapter are included in the chapter's Creative Commons license, unless indicated otherwise in a credit line to the material. If material is not included in the chapter's Creative Commons license and your intended use is not permitted by statutory regulation or exceeds the permitted use, you will need to obtain permission directly from the copyright holder.

Index

A
Absolute right
  absolutist, 28
Abstract logic
  abstraction, 15, 54, 55
Africa
  Africans, 44
Alienability, 12, 13, 15, 61
Americas, 3, 19, 44
  America, 19
Amerindian, 45, 46, 48
Anglo-Saxon, 8, 10, 11, 33

B
Bentham, Jeremy, 34, 48
Blackstone, William, 4, 15, 27–34, 54, 55, 62, 65
British Empire, 19, 46

C
Capitalism
  capital, 20, 37–39, 44, 47, 48, 55
Caribbean, 3, 43–48, 55
Climate change, 3
Colonialism, 40, 46
Common heritage of mankind, 61
Common law, 2–4, 7, 10, 13–15, 17, 25, 29, 31–33, 35, 48, 54, 63, 65, 66
Commons, 12, 14, 18–25, 28, 32, 33, 54, 55, 65, 66

Custom
  Customary law, 9–11, 14, 15, 18, 30, 31, 61, 63, 65

D
Dephysicalisation, 37, 43
Dunbar-Ortiz, Roxanne, 24

E
Enclosure, 14, 18–21, 23, 24, 29, 32, 34, 65, 66
Enclosure Acts, 33, 54
England, 2, 8, 10–14, 18–21, 24, 28, 31–33, 47, 48, 54, 55
Exclusion, 19, 27, 28, 60

F
Famine, 10, 41–43, 48
Feudalism, 9, 54, 55
  feudal pyramid, 30, 32

G
Graham, Nicole, 4, 8, 12, 13, 18, 19, 29, 32, 33, 38–40, 43, 44, 46, 48

H
Hardin, Garret, 54
Hohfeld, Wesley Newcomb, 34, 48

© The Editor(s) (if applicable) and The Author(s) 2023
A. Byer, *Placing Property*, Palgrave Socio-Legal Studies,
https://doi.org/10.1007/978-3-031-31994-5

Homogenisation, 17

I
Improvement
 Improvement theory, 19, 20, 24, 33, 54
Indigenous, 4, 20, 23–25, 56, 61
Ireland, 3, 10, 40–43, 55, 62

L
Labour theory of value, 18, 27
Land, 1, 2, 8, 9, 11, 13, 19, 21, 31, 55, 63
Landscape, 3, 4, 8–10, 12–15, 17, 19, 23, 24, 30, 32, 34, 38–40, 42, 43, 45, 47–49, 54–56, 61, 63, 65–67
Legal geography, 1, 3, 4, 48, 62
Locke, John, 4, 7, 15, 17–25, 27, 54, 65

M
Marx, Karl, 4, 15, 37–44, 48, 49, 54, 55, 65
Metabolic rift, 38, 55
Monoculture, 42

N
Native
 Native American, 19
Nature, 2, 9, 12, 15, 18–21, 23, 25, 28, 38–40, 43, 44, 46, 48, 49, 55, 66
Norman
 Norman conquest, 8, 10, 12, 14, 29, 30, 32, 33, 55

O
Olwig, Kenneth, 8–10, 12–15, 20, 32, 44, 56, 61
Ownership, 1–3, 8, 10, 12–15, 17–19, 23, 29, 30, 32–34, 38, 39, 44, 47, 48, 56, 59, 60, 62, 63, 66

P
Place, 3, 8, 12–15, 19, 22, 32, 35, 43, 47, 55, 61, 62, 65
Placelessness, 65
Progressive Property, 59
Property, 1–4, 7, 8, 11–13, 15, 17–25, 27–34, 37–40, 42, 43, 46–49, 53–55, 59–63, 65–67

R
Rose, Carol, 25, 28, 54, 62
Rundale, 10, 40, 41, 43

S
Slave colonies
 slavery, 43, 44, 47
Spatial justice, 4, 54, 60
Spatial logic, 15

T
Tenures, 3, 30, 31, 54
Tragedy of the Commons, 54

W
Wales, 20
Waste, 18, 20, 21, 25
Wilderness, 23–25, 56

Ingram Content Group UK Ltd.
Milton Keynes UK
UKHW020059040723
424518UK00005B/289